# SWING WIN

## TORNADOS, TOMCATS AND BACKFIRES

# SWING WINGS

## TORNADOS, TOMCATS AND BACKFIRES

Tim Laming

First published in Great Britain in 1993
by Osprey, an imprint of Reed Consumer Books
Limited
Michelin House, 81 Fulham Road,
London SW3 6RB
and Auckland, Melbourne, Singapore and
Toronto

ISBN 1 85532 3737

Edited by Tony Holmes
Page design by Paul Kime
Printed in Hong Kong

# Acknowledgements

The following illustrations represent a general overview of the variety of variable geometry combat aircraft designs which are currently in service around the world. Many of the photographs were taken by myself, and I must thank one or two individuals who enabled me to be in the right place at the right time in order to press my camera's shutter button. In particular I must thank Michael Hill and Dale Donovan at RAF Strike Command, the staff of the Public Affair Office at Edwards AFB, and the Public Affairs Officers at NAS Oceana, and NAS Patuxent River.

Other photographs were kindly supplied by my illustrious colleagues, to whom I extend my sincere gratitude, and again I must thank a few individuals, these being: Frank Visser, Boudewijn Pieters, Giuseppe Fassari, Andy Hodgson, Scott Van Aken, Gary Meinert, Martin Bowman, Peter Foster, and Joel Paskauskas. Thanks guys! I hope you like the results!

Tim Laming.

**Title page** Heads down! An intimate view of a Tornado F.3, with landing gear and flaps extended, about to touch-down at RAF Coningsby. Note the empty Skyflash missile bays (*Photo by Tim Laming*)

**Above** F-111A 66-022 is now preserved at the entrance to Mountain Home AFB, Idaho, in dramatic flying configuration. However, the F-111 has long since departed from Mountain Home, and the base is now occupied by B-52s, F-15s and F-16s as part of Air Combat Command's Composite Wing concept *(Photo by Scott Van Aken)*

# Introduction

Combat aircraft design is a complicated process, requiring huge numbers of man-hours to produce designs which meet military requirements. Unfortunately, no aircraft can ever be completely 'perfect', as each design has to be capable of meeting a range of aerodynamic requirements, some of which conflict directly with each other. For example, a fighter may be 'built for speed', but manoeuvrability is important too, and designing an aircraft to achieve both aims is, to say the least, difficult.

It is with this point in mind that designers began to look at the concept of variable-geometry, or 'swing wings'. Precisely who was first responsible for this ingenious invention is difficult to establish, but Barnes Wallis was certainly a pioneer in this field, producing a number of aerodynamic design models, some of which flew quite successfully. But of course, like most ingenious British designs, it never resulted in an operational aircraft design.

It was the United States Air Force which first adopted the operational swing wing aircraft, in the shape of the General Dynamics YF-111A, which flew for the first time on 21 December 1964. Originally a joint USAF/Navy programme, the latter soon abandoned its interest in the F-111, but the aircraft was nevertheless developed into a hugely successful tactical strike aircraft which, 30 years later, is still more than a match for any other comparable design. The swing wing design enables the F-111 to achieve a speed of Mach 2.5, whilst still maintaining a very respectable range (almost 3000 miles), and a comfortably slow landing speed. In many respects, the concept of variable geometry has enabled the aerodynamicist to incorporate conflicting requirements into one very flexible design.

Of course, the Soviets were not too far behind the Americans in terms of swing wing technology, and the prototype Mikoyan-Gurevich MiG-23 (known as the Ye-231) was first seen in 1967. The *Flogger* became a first class fighter-bomber, as did the Sukhoi Su-17, which appeared at approximately the same time as the MiG-23. The Soviets continued to develop swing wing designs, which led to the Su-24 *Fencer* and Tu-22 *Backfire,* together with what is presumably the ultimate Russian variable-geometry aircraft, the mighty Tu-160 *Blackjack.*

However, developments in the United States continued apace, resulting in the production of the Grumman F-14 Tomcat, still regarded as one of the most effective and successful fighter designs, despite having first flown way back in 1970. Over 20 years later, swing wings are still very much in business, and as the venerable B-52 reaches retirement, the spearhead of Air Combat Command's nuclear strike force is now the Rockwell B-1B Lancer, an aircraft which has suffered more than its fair share of technical 'teething problems', but is still undoubtedly the most formidable bomber to have ever been built.

Meanwhile, across the Atlantic in Europe, the multi-national MRCA (Multi Role Combat Aircraft) was developed into the hugely successful Tornado interdictor/strike aircraft, and the rather less-breathtaking air defence variant, which illustrates that even variable geometry can not perform miracles! The 1991 Gulf War was the Tornado's baptism of fire, and the Royal Air Force quickly emphasised just how effective the Tornado IDS really is.

However, aircraft design continues to evolve, and the swing wing concept (at least in the currently-recognisable form) has probably been developed as far as is practically possible – recent aerodynamic design has switched to other more effective ways of 'achieving the impossible'. For the foreseeable future, however, the Tornado, Tomcat, F-111, Lancer, *Blackjack, Flogger, Fitter* and *Fencer* are destined to continue in military service around the world, until better and even more bizarre designs come along.

# Contents

**Above** This MiG-23UB was operated by the 787th Fighter Regiment in a training capacity, alongside the unit's more common MiG-29 *Fulcrums*. Photographed at Finow-Eberswalde during June 1992, the aircraft's peculiar camouflage colours were applied with hand-brushes, using paint that is normally reserved for the aircraft shelter doors! *(Photo by F Visser/M Tabak)*

# F-111 'Aardvark'

Although something of a 'vintage' combat aircraft, having first entered service with the USAF during 1967, the General Dynamics F-111 is still very much 'in business', albeit in slowly diminishing numbers. The origins of this famous bomber can be traced back to 1961, when a TFX (Tactical Fighter, Experimental) was first issued in an effort to produce a multi-role fighter-bomber for service with both the USAF and the Navy. Although the navalised development did not proceed beyond the prototype stage, the land-based F-111A joined Tactical Air Command (TAC) in June 1967, and less than a year later, aircraft were deployed to Vietnam. This first operational deployment was less-than successful, and it was only during a second tour of duty from 1972 onwards that the aircraft was given a proper opportunity to prove its effectiveness.

The basic early production model, the F-111A, was later joined by the F-111E, which was essentially an improved version of the A-model. The engine intakes were enlarged in order to accommodate Pratt & Whitney TF30-P-100 engines, although these powerplants were only fitted at a later stage to the F-111F. The E-model was delivered to the 20th Tactical Fighter Wing (TFW) at RAF Upper Heyford during September 1970, and this variant continued to serve with the 20th TFW almost exclusively until 1992, when the gradual wind-down of this unit began (leading to the eventual closure of Upper Heyford as an operational USAF base).

The next variant (although out of sequence) was the F-111D, which entered service in October 1971 at Cannon AFB in New Mexico. The D-model was almost a 'second generation' aircraft, with a completely new avionics package and a Head Up Display (HUD) for both the pilot and WSO (Weapons System Operator). The F-111D was widely regarded as the best of the F-111 variants in terms of overall performance, but despite this, the D-model has continued to operate exclusively in the training role. The F-111F was the ultimate development of the basic airframe, with uprated TF30-P-100 engines giving the aircraft a very respectable reserve of power. Delivered initially to Mountain Home AFB in Idaho, the F-111Fs were later deployed to England, joining the 48th TFW at RAF Lakenheath, where they

**Left** Take a long drive out into the Californian Desert, and eventually you will arrive at Edwards AFB, the spiritual birthplace of American military aviation. Situated between the security outpost and the main base entrance is a small collection of former test aircraft, including a rare grey/white F-111A *(Photo by Tim Laming)*

**Above** F-111D from the 522nd Fighter Squadron, based at Cannon AFB. The 'standard' F-111 South-east Asian brown/green camouflage is now being progressively replaced by what appears to be Air Combat Command's 'corporate livery' of overall Gunship Gray *(Photo by Gary Meinert)*

**Left** SAC, together with its FB-111As, is now long-gone, and although many of the aircraft have re-entered service with Air Combat Command as F-111Gs, older airframes have been retired. One aircraft has survived to join numerous other former SAC machines at March AFB in California, where a fascinating museum collection of combat aircraft is maintained. The view beyond the FB-111 evokes memories of even earlier days, when the B-47 was SAC's main airborne nuclear deterrent *(Photo by Tim Laming)*

remained in service until 1992/93, when F-15E Strike Eagles were delivered as replacements.

The F-111, better known as the 'Aardvark' by air and ground crews alike, continued to be developed, and while TAC took deliveries of the basic fighter-bomber variant, Strategic Air Command received a total of 76 FB-111As, a strategic bomber development with a longer wing span and a modified weapons system, which could accommodate nuclear bombs. Entering service at Plattsburgh AFB, New York, in 1969, the FB-111A was capable of carrying a range of nuclear weapons, and continued in service almost until the last days of Strategic Air Command's existance. Some of these airframes were then 'conventionalized' and transferred to TAC

**Above** Taxying in to Westfield ANGB in Massachusetts after a long cross-country flight, a 27th FW F-111D heads for the transient ramp. Some 96 D-models were constructed, all of which were powered by two Pratt & Whitney TF30-P-9 turbofans. The F-111's maximum speed is in excess of Mach 2 *(Photo by Tim Laming)*

**Left** Decorated by a collection of 'Remove Before Flight' tags and air intake covers, a 27th Fighter Wing F-111D rests between sorties. Most 'Aardvark' pilots consider the D-model to be the best F-111 variant, with good all-round attack and air combat capabilities. Despite this high praise, the variant has remained in use as an operational conversion trainer throughout its career *(Photo by Tim Laming)*

(now Air Combat Command), who re-designated it the F-111G.

The Royal Australian Air Force are the only other users of the aircraft, receiving 24 F-111Cs in 1973 (and about a dozen attrition replacements over the ensuing two decades), although the RAF almost became an F-111 operator after the British government ordered the type following cancellation of the TSR.2. In typical fashion, the government later changed course yet again, cancelling the order for F-111Ks, and purchasing F-4K/M Phantom IIs instead.

Certainly the most heavily modified 'Aardvark' variant is the EF-111A Raven, developed by Grumman Aerospace, who utilised F-111A airframes. A total of 42 aircraft were modified to this standard, and now serve with

Air Combat Command in the defence suppression role, fitted with an ALQ-99E tactical jamming system developed from the package used by the US Navy's EA-6B Prowler.

Although the F-111 first saw operational service in Vietnam, it was during 1986 that the aircraft achieved worldwide recognition when the 48th TFW spearheaded a large-scale night attack on targets in Libya, under the codename Operation *Eldorado Canyon*. The F-111F later went to war again during 1991 as part of Operation *Desert Storm*. The 48th TFW again provided the main F-111 force, deploying their F-models to Taif in Saudi Arabia, where they joined a number of EF-111A aircraft, which supported numerous Allied strike 'packages' as they flew over Iraq. The 20th TFW also deployed F-111Es to Incirlik in Turkey as part of the offensive, and together, the F-111 force flew over 4000 sorties during *Desert Storm*.

**Above** The 57th Fighter Weapons Wing, based at McClellan AFB in California, has operated a number of F-111 variants usually from Nellis AFB in Nevada. 67-120 is an F-111E, wearing old-style white 'WA' tail codes and South-east Asian camouflage, with the familiar Nevada mountains in the background *(Photo by Andy Hodgson collection)*

**Above** Pictured during a refuelling stopover at Norton AFB in California, F-111A 67-095 was pictured during March 1990, when the aircraft was operated by the 391st Tactical Fighter Squadron, at Mountain Home AFB, Idaho. Note the Tactical Air Command badge on the tail *(Photo by Scott Van Aken)*

The F-111 has a huge weapons-carrying capability and is able to deliver virtually every weapon in the USAF's inventory. As well as possessing the option of fitting an internally-mounted 20 mm cannon, the aircraft also enjoys a further eight weapons stations to which a variety of stores can be attached, including retarded and 'slick' bombs, cluster bomb units (CBUs), the GBU-15 glide bomb, laser guided bombs (the F-111F normally being equipped with a Paveway laser designator in the weapons bay), and self-defence Sidewinder missiles. Nuclear bombs and a variety of self-defence ECM (Electronic Counter Measures) pods can also be carried. Perhaps the most unusual weapon to have been carried so far is the hastily-developed GBU-28 4700 lb bomb, which was dropped twice during *Desert Storm* as a 'bunker-buster'. Although one drop was unsuccessful, the second sortie destroyed an underground Iraqi command bunker.

As deliveries of F-15E Strike Eagles continue, the F-111 force is slowly contracting and concentrating at Cannon AFB in New Mexico. The F-111G (formerly SAC's FB-111As) has largely been replaced by deliveries of F-111Es from England, and likewise, the F-111A and F-111D are to be replaced by the F-111F, which has also re-located from England. Although once referred to as 'McNamara's folly', the F-111 is now widely regarded as an excellent strike aircraft, and despite the continuing deliveries of Strike Eagles, the Aardvark is expected to continue in service with Air Combat Command for many years. Likewise, the Royal Australian Air Force's F-111C fleet is expected to remain active for some considerable time (augmented by deliveries of former USAF airframes), and the EF-111A Raven (often referred to as the 'Spark Vark') is to be upgraded in order to maintain its capability throughout the 1990s.

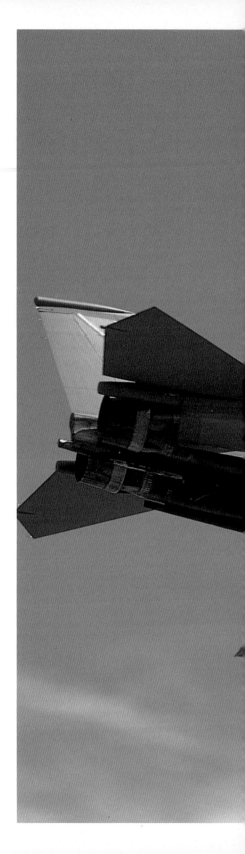

## F-111E

**Wing:** span 63 ft 0 in (19.20 m) spread and 31 ft 11.4 in (9.74 m) swept; area 525.0 sq ft (48.77 m²) spread and 683.3 sq ft (61.07m²) swept

**Fuselage and tail:** length 73 ft 6 in (22.40 m); height 17 ft 1.4 in (5.22 m)

**Powerplant:** two Pratt & Whitney TF30-P-3 turbofans each rated at 18,500 lbs (82.29kN) afterburning thrust

**Weights:** operating empty 46,172 lb (20,943 kg); maximum take-off 91,300 lbs (41,414 kg)

**Fuel and load:** internal fuel 5033 US gal (19,052 litres); external fuel up to four 600-US gal (2271 litre) drop tanks; maximum ordnance 31,500 lbs

**Speed:** maximum level speed 'clean' at 36,000 ft (10,975 m) 1650 mph (2655 km/h); cruising speed at high altitude 571 mph (919 km/h)

**Range:** maximum range with full internal fuel more than 2925 miles (4707 km)

**Performance:** service ceiling 60,000 ft (18,290 m); take-off distance to 50 ft (15 m) 3120 ft (950 m); landing distance less than 3000 ft (915 m)

**Right** Unusual underside view, illustrating the gloss red flap interior, an under-fuselage AXX-14 data link pod, together with practice bombs, AIM-9 Sidewinder AAM and an instrumentation pod under the wings (*Photo by Boudewijn Pieters*)

**Above** Public flight demonstrations by the F-111 have never been exactly common. During one of RAF Upper Heyford's last public events before the base ceased flight operations, four F-111Es from the 20th TFW rumble overhead, displaying four wing-sweep positions. Try that in an F-15E! *(Photo by Tim Laming)*

**Right** F-111E down in the dirt, thundering through the smoke and debris created by a four-ship simulated attack. The 'Aardvark' has demonstrated (over Libya and Iraq) its excellent capabilities as an all-weather night attack aircraft *(Photo by Tim Laming)*

**Above** EF-111A Raven, wearing the Mountain Home AFB's 'MO' tail code. These Idaho-based aircraft have now relocated to Cannon AFB, and Mountain Home AFB is now home to Air Combat Command's first complete Composite Wing *(Photo by Curtiss Knowles)*

**Left** An Upper Heyford-based EF-111 sweeps over the runway threshold at RAF Fairford in Gloucestershire, carrying an underwing luggage pod ready for a long weekend stay at the 1991 International Air Tattoo. This side profile illustrates the main landing gear door which, when extended, acts as a very effective air brake *(Photo by Boudewijn Pieters)*

# F-14 Tomcat

The Grumman F-14 Tomcat is without doubt one of the most effective (and most expensive) fighter aircraft currently in military service. It is perhaps a little surprising to note that it first entered service with the US Navy some 20 years ago, yet despite this, the aircraft is still as potent as ever. A total of 28 Navy squadrons currently operate the Tomcat, together with various test establishments and Iran, who was the solitary export customer for the aircraft.

A true air superiority fighter, the F-14 is primarily operated as a defender of the naval battlegroup, providing a defensive screen well beyond the area in which the vessels operate. Flying combat air patrols (CAPs) under the direction of E-2C Hawkeye Airborne Early Warning directors, the Tomcat crews are able to maintain air superiority over an area which will often extend up to 400 miles from the parent aircraft carrier.

The F-14's weapons system is built around the Hughes AWG-9 radar 'package', which includes a television camera system (TCS) and secure datalink facilities. The radar scanner is a multi-mode unit with a range of approximately 150 miles and a capability to track up to 24 individual targets at any given time. The computer system is programmed to prioritize targets depending on their closure-rate, enabling the Tomcat's Radar Intercept Officer (RIO) to determine which contacts pose the most serious threat to either the F-14, or the battlegroup it is defending.

The main weapon utilised by the Tomcat is the Hughes AIM-54C Phoenix, a very sophisticated and hugely expensive missile, which has demonstrated an excellent range capability (in excess of 90 miles), but to date has not been fired operationally. The Phoenix has an internal active radar seeker, which makes the missile a 'fire and forget' weapon, adding an even greater 'kill capability' to the overall F-14 weapons system. The solid-state radar and internal target detecting devices (TDDs) enable the Phoenix to tackle any type of aerial target, at high or low altitude, and even cruise missiles. Although the Tomcat can carry six AIM-54s, the 983 lb weight of each missile usually restricts the maximum load to just two, allowing the pilot to execute more 'comfortable' arrested landings on board the aircraft carrier.

**Right** Keeping the Tomcats clean is a nice idea, but not the main priority as members of Oceana's groundcrew brave the heat to wash-down one of the 'Grim Reaper's' birds. Because almost every training mission takes the aircraft out over the Atlantic, the salt-laden atmosphere presents a potential corrosion problem which needs to be addressed as regularly as possible by the thorough rinsing away of salt deposits *(Photo by Tim Laming)*

**Above** 'Hi Mom!' One member of the crew certainly possesses good situational awareness, having spotted the cameraman as he walks-out to his Tomcat parked on Oceana's flightline. His bonedome is protected by a rather stylish *Desert Storm* cover *(Photo by Tim Laming)*

**Left** What better place to wait for your playmates than up on the fuselage of your very own 'mean machine'? The pilot and RIO wait for their fellow flyers before departing on an ACM training exercise, on a hot July morning in 1992 *(Photo by Tim Laming)*

For medium range interceptions, the F-14 normally carries a pair of Raytheon AIM-7M Sparrow missiles. The Sparrow is a semi-active radar homing missile, which in its original AAM-N-6 form dates back to 1951! However, the latest Mike version bears little resemblance to its ancestor, the weapon possessing an excellent BVR (Beyond Visual Range) capability – the only disadvantage associated with the missile is that the aircraft must illuminate the target with its radar until the point of impact. Development of a new medium range weapon is continuing, and the Hughes AIM-120 AMRAAM (Advanced Medium Range Air-to-Air Missile) will incorporate an active radar seeker, allowing the Tomcat to launch the missile and either retreat to safety, or engage other targets. The AIM-120 is also much lighter than the Sparrow, enabling the missile to be carried even on Sidewinder launch stations. Production of the AIM-120 began (after many delays) during 1992, and deliveries are now getting underway.

**Above** Tomcats from VF-102 'Diamondbacks' were deployed on board the USS *America* (CV-66) during *Desert Storm*, returning to Oceana later in 1991. Twelve months down the road, 'AG/111' is pictured back home in Virginia after returning from an early morning training mission out over the Atlantic *(Photo by Tim Laming)*

**Left** Out under the blistering sun, the groundcrew are hard at work on Oceana's flightline, replacing a VF-33 Tomcat's Hughes AWG-9 radar dish *(Photo by Tim Laming)*

For short range engagements, the Tomcat also carries a pair of Ford Aerospace/Raytheon AIM-9M Sidewinder missiles, this weapon being perhaps the most famous air-to-air weapon ever developed. The Mike version is also a much-developed model of an older design which, like the Sparrow, dates back to 1951. The original Sidewinder was a much less capable weapon, which could only be successfully fired from directly behind a non-manoeuvring aircraft at very close range. The Mike, however, is an all-aspect missile with five times the range of its ancestor. Fitted as 'standard' to almost every current fighter/attack aircraft within the Western World, the AIM-9 has been used operationally in many aerial conflicts, including *Desert Storm*. Development of the missile continues, and an improved version, the AIM-9R, is now being introduced. In addition to the Sidewinder, the Tomcat's close-in combat capability is augmented by a built-in 20 mm Vulcan cannon.

**Above** Not the most colourful of paint schemes, but certainly an eye-catcher, this VF-33 'Starfighters' machine was photographed whilst undergoing line maintenance at NAS Oceana during July 1992. Oceana is a great place for aircraft spotters, with a well-placed recreation park from where dozens of Tomcats, Skyhawks, Tiger IIs and Fighting Falcons can be seen wheeling around the sky almost every day. And Virginia Beach is just a few minutes away. Sounds like heaven! *(Photo by Tim Laming)*

**Right** Access doors open, a pair of Tomcats await attention from Oceana's maintenance men. Although low-vis grey camouflage is applied to most aircraft, it is still part of US Navy policy to paint the edges of doors and other moveable items with gloss red paint as a safety measure
*(Photo by Tim Laming)*

**Above** Sweet nostalgia! A 1977-vintage view of an F-14A from VF-32 at NAS Oceana, illustrating the original post-delivery white/grey Tomcat paint scheme, full colour national insignia and high-visibility unit markings. Not a single concession to tactical camouflage in sight, but what a great way to encourage esprit de corps within a military fighting unit *(Photo by Joe Paskauskas collection)*

**Left** Oceana's groundcrew carefully tow an F-14 from the servicing hangar out into the Virginia sunshine to join the lines of assembled Tomcats. NAS Oceana is one of the US Navy's busiest airfields, and the home of the Atlantic Fleet Tomcat squadrons *(Photo by Tim Laming)*

Three basic versions of the Tomcat are currently operated by the US Navy. The F-14A is the original production variant, powered by Pratt & Whitney TF30-P-414A turbofans. Problems with the TF30 powerplant led to the replacement of early versions of the engine, although even in its latest modification state, it is far from ideal, being prone to compressor stalls. The F-14B (originally known as the F-14A Plus) is essentially a basic A-model, but with General Electric F110-GE-400 turbofans, which are much more powerful and 'user friendly'. Some new-build F-14Bs were delivered (38 in total), while others were converted from F-14As (a further 32). The ultimate Tomcat variant is the F-14D, which also uses the General Electric F110, but is also fitted with an updated avionics suite, including an AN/APG-71 radar. As with the F-14B, some D-models have been

**Above** No chance of mis-identifying this Tomcat as one of the 'Swordsmen', better known as VF-32. When the unit is not deployed on board the USS *John F Kennedy* (CV-67), home base is NAS Oceana, where BuNo 162701 was photographed in July 1992 *(Photo by Tim Laming)*

**Left** Although this is a Miramar-based F-14, the photograph was taken at NAF El Centro out in the Californian desert. Although El Centro is best known as the winter home of the Blue Angels, the base also plays host to other US Navy aircraft, and Tomcats deploy from Miramar almost on a daily basis to fly ACM missions in the relatively uncluttered airspace out over the desert *(Photo by Tim Laming)*

manufactured from scratch (37 aircraft), the last being completed during 1992. However, further examples will be converted from A-models in due course, although the number is likely to be very small.

Although the Tomcat continues to operate almost exclusively as a dedicated dogfighter, the aircraft can attack as well as defend. Trials during 1990 demonstrated that the F-14 can deliver bombs, and both the F-14B and F-14D incorporate air-to-ground delivery software into their weapons systems. As a result of this 'new found' ability, the B- and D-equipped units fly a limited number of air-to-ground training missions, although Tomcats have not been flown operationally in this role so far.

Tactical reconnaissance is also undertaken by some F-14 squadrons, and a number of Tomcats are continually configured to carry TARPS (Tactical

**Above** F-14A from VF-51 'Screaming Eagles', deployed on-board the USS *Kitty Hawk* (CV-63), returns to NAS Miramar while the carrier is docked just 'down the road' at NAS North Island in San Diego. The aircraft wears a peculiar mix of low-vis squadron markings, and high-vis national insignia *(Photo by Tim Laming)*

**Above right** The oblique evening sunlight illustrates quite clearly that Miramar's Tomcats are fitted with Goodyear tyres! The Miramar airfield circuit is almost continually busy, not only with home-based F-14s, Hawkeyes, Greyhounds, Skyhawks and F-16s, but also a wide range of visiting types too, including USAF aircraft, which regularly deploy to Miramar for dissimilar air combat training *(Photo by Tim Laming)*

**Right** Although the US Navy's Pacific Fleet Tomcats are largely camouflaged, some aircraft are an exception to the rule. After a long, long wait on a hot and dusty San Diego freeway, the unmistakable shape of VF-111's brilliantly-painted F-14A came into view, bringing back fond memories of a past era when every Navy combat aircraft was worth a second glance *(Photo by Tim Laming)*

Air Reconnaissance Pod System) under the aircraft fuselage. Indeed, the system was used operationally during *Desert Storm* in 1991, and one unfortunate crew from VF-103 'Sluggers' was shot down by an Iraqi SA-2 *Guideline* surface-to-air missile whilst flying a reconnaissance mission. Luckily both crew members survived the incident, which was to be the only Tomcat loss throughout the entire war.

The F-14 also went into action during August 1981, when two VF-41 'Black Aces' aircraft destroyed a pair of Libyan Su-22 *Fitters* during an engagement over the Gulf of Sidra. Tomcats also provided air cover when the United States launched an attack on Libya in April 1986, and more recently, played an important part in *Desert Storm*, as well as relief operations in Somalia during 1992/93.

## Grumman F-14B Tomcat

**Wing:** span (20 degree sweep), 64 ft 1.5 in (19.55 m); (68 degree sweep) 37 ft 7 in (11.45 m); wing area 565 sq ft (52.50 m²)

**Fuselage and tail:** length 61 ft 12 in (18.90 m); height 16 ft 0 in (4.88 m)

**Powerplant:** two General Electric F110-GE-400 turbofans each rated at 27,080 lb afterburning thrust

**Weights:** empty 42,000 lbs (19,050 kg); max take-off 75,000 lbs (34,020 kg)

Max speed (with four semi-recessed AIM-7 missiles) 912 mph (1468 km/h) at sea level, or Mach 1.2 (1544 mph/2485 km/h) at 40,000 ft (12,190 m)

**Range:** combat air patrol loiter time (with two 267 US gal/1011 litre external tanks) 2.7 hours; intercept radius at Mach 1.3, 510 miles 820 km)

**Right** Engines throttled back and wings swept, a Tomcat streaks in from Miramar to begin an impressive display routine at MCAS El Toro. F-14 demonstrations are understandably very popular in the US, and quite common too, whereas the appearance of a Tomcat in Europe is always a rather special event. Let's hope that situation does not last forever! *(Photo by Tim Laming)*

**Above** The last Tomcat left Grumman's production line in 1992, and already some early-build F-14As are amongst the ranks of externally stored airframes at Davis-Monthan AFB in Arizona, carefully preserved with applications of spray-on latex protective film (known as 'Spraylat')
*(Photo by Boudewijn Pieters)*

**Left** F-14A from VF-211 'Checkmates' on final approach to NAS Miramar. The ultra-low visibility markings are applied to many Tomcats, but as time goes by, more and more aircraft are re-appearing with more flamboyant colours. Camouflage may be effective, but boy is it boring!
*(Photo by Tim Laming)*

# Soviet Swingers

While the United States was busy developing swing wing technology, the Soviets, as ever, were not far behind, and during the 1960s they also produced the first of a series of variable-geometry fighter and bomber designs. Rather than designing a new swing wing ground attack aircraft from scratch, Pavel Sukhoi's design bureau opted to re-design an existing airframe, the Sukhoi Su-7, which had been developed some years earlier. Almost as soon as the original Su-7 had entered service, it became clear that the aircraft suffered from a restricted weapons load and range, and by re-designing the outer wing sections to pivot, the aircraft would be able to achieve much greater lift, and thus be equipped to carry more fuel, whilst retaining a high speed capability.

The first suitably modified aircraft appeared in public during the 1967 Aviation Day at Moscow's Domodyedovo Airport, and as the aircraft was clearly not representative of a production machine, Western analysts quickly dismissed it as little more than a novelty. Of course, it was something more than that, and the swing wing Su-17 is still very much in service a quarter of a century later. The aircraft was exported to Poland, Czechoslovakia, Egypt, Angola, Libya, Peru, Afghanistan and Algeria, under the designations Su-20 and Su-22. Given the NATO codename *Fitter*, the type was also a major component of the now-defunct East German Air Force, and following the reunification of East and West Germany, many Su-22s received Luftwaffe serials, continuing to fly in a non-operational status for a short while, before the entire fleet was placed in storage. A few examples of these aircraft were distributed to various test and research establishments, including Boscombe Down (and later Farnborough) in England.

Almost in parallel with Sukhoi's efforts, Mikoyan-Gurevich developed a new fighter-bomber aircraft, based on their experience with the MiG-21 design. However, rather than revising an existing aircraft (as Sukhoi had done), the prototype Ye-231 was a completely new design, which first appeared in public at the same Aviation Day as the new Sukhoi in 1957. With full-span variable-geometry wings and shoulder-mounted air intakes, the new aircraft was something of a radical departure from previous

**Right** Sukhoi Su-17M-4 from the 20th Fighter Bomber Regiment at Templin during 1992. The 20th was the only Fitter Regiment to operate in the former German Democratic Republic before returning to Russia in 1993. The Guard Regiment badge on the nose of '04' indicates that the unit dates back to World War 2 *(Photo by F Visser/M Tabak)*

## Sukhoi Su-17

**Wing:** 45 ft 11.2 in
**Fuselage and tail:** length 61 ft 6.2 in; height 15 ft 7.0 in
**Powerplant:** one Lyulka AL-21F-3 turbojet rated at 24,690 lb (with afterburning)
**Speed:** 1380 mph (estimated)
**Range:** 390 miles (estimated)
**Weight:** 39,022 lbs (estimated)

designs, but despite its then-unusual appearance, the jet was successfully developed into the MiG-23 and MiG-27 series of fighter-bombers, which continue to serve with a large number of military air arms around the world. With the NATO codename *Flogger,* the swing wing MiG-23/27 is now a familiar sight to Western observers, former East German examples having been examined by various research establishments, while Czechoslovakian examples have even ventured to some overseas air shows, including events in England.

While the Su-17 and MiG-23 represent the first generation of Soviet swing wing aircraft, a new variable-geometry combat design was first observed during the early 1970s, and is now recognised as a Russian equivalent to the F-111 and Tornado. The Sukhoi Su-24, with the NATO codename *Fencer,* first entered service during 1974 as a low-level strike/attack bomber, with all-weather and night attack capabilities. Like America's F-111, the two-man crew are seated in a rather cramped side-by-side cockpit, with ejection seats rather than an escape capsule. Although the main Su-24 force has remained primarily within Russian boundaries throughout the *Fencer's* career, small numbers of Su-24s were based in East Germany until 1992, when the last few aircraft returned home to Russia. The once-secret aircraft has also made a few public appearances, a brightly-decorated demonstration aircraft appearing at the 1992 SBAC Farnborough show.

On a much grander scale, Tupolev also embraced the variable-geometry concept in an effort to extend the capabilities of the Tu-22 bomber. With a range of less than 2000 miles, the original *Blinder* was something less than a truly strategic bomber, and during the mid-1960s, the Tupolev bureau began work on a re-designed aircraft which featured a new wing configuration and engine layout – the end result was a virtually all-new design known as the Tu-22M (and the later Tu-26/28), with the NATO

**Left** With its wings swept fully forward and trailing-edge flaps and leading-edge slats extended, a 20th Fighter Bomber Regiment Su-17M-4 powers by on final approach to Templin during August 1992 *(Photo by F Visser/M Tabak)*

**Above** With both the front and rear canopy closed, the Su-22M-3 does assume a fairly graceful appearance. Here, '07' takes a well-earned rest at Taszar during August 1991. The second *Fitter* to the right illustrates the considerable difference in camouflage demarcation and colour application throughout the Hungarian fleet. In the distance a line of MiG-21 *Fishbeds* are visible *(Photo by Peter Foster)*

**Left** Pictured at Finow during August 1991, this Sukhoi Su-17M wears an unusual light brown/green camouflage scheme. The Su-17 was developed from the fixed-geometry Su-7, and approximately 700 aircraft were produced for ground attack operations with the former Soviet Air Force. A further 150 were produced for tactical reconnaissance duties *(Photo by Peter Foster)*

codename *Backfire*. First observed by reconnaissance satellites during 1969, the type is now established in service with both the Russian Air Force and Navy. The first major public appearance took place in September 1992 when a Tu-22M flew to Farnborough to participate in the bi-annual SBAC show. Only a few years previously, the *Backfire* represented the spearhead of the Warsaw Pact's offensive nuclear strike force, and now, in 1992, the huge swing wing bomber was casually performing before the British public. Times really have changed!

If anything of the former Soviet Air Force remains shrouded in mystery, then perhaps Tupolev's ultimate bomber design fits that category. The huge Tu-160, codenamed *Blackjack*, is the Russian equivalent of the

**Above** A former JBG 77 aircraft, Su-22U '25+54' was photographed at Laage during July 1991, where it shows little evidence of its former East German markings. The four underwing gun pods are clearly evident, and a well-camouflaged aircraft shelter is visible behind the *Fitter*
*(Photo by F Visser/M Tabak)*

**Left** Theoretically speaking, this Sukhoi Su-22M-4 was part of NATO when this photograph was taken in 1991. Although the *Fitter-K* was not incorporated into the united Luftwaffe, the Sukhoi-designed fighter-bomber remained present in the former East Germany until 1992, despite its operational flying having effectively ceased when the two Germany's merged in October 1990. Sadly, '546' never appeared at a NATO Tiger Meet, despite wearing some very eye-catching feline decorations, as part of JBG 77 at Laage
*(Photo by F Visser/M Tabak)*

**USAF's B-1 Lancer, with a remarkably similar layout, albeit slightly larger. The Tu-160 has appeared at Russian air shows, but has yet to make any public appearance further afield. Production of the relatively new bomber has now been halted, and only about 40 aircraft have actually achieved operational status. In view of their rather costly nature, and continuing strategic arms reductions, their operational future does not seem too secure.**

**Above** Some eye-catching markings were applied to JG 9's MiG-23ML '20+26' shortly before the type was withdrawn from use. Photographed in July 1991, the aircraft has now been disposed of and Peenemünde's MiGs have all long since departed *(Photo by F Visser/M Tabak)*

**Right** MiG-23MLD *Flogger* departing from Alteslager for the last time, en-route for Russia. The underwing and under-fuselage long-range fuel tanks are visible, these stores being necessary for a long ferry flight from East Germany. Also visible on top of the fuselage are chaff and flare dispensers *(Photo by F Visser/M Tabak)*

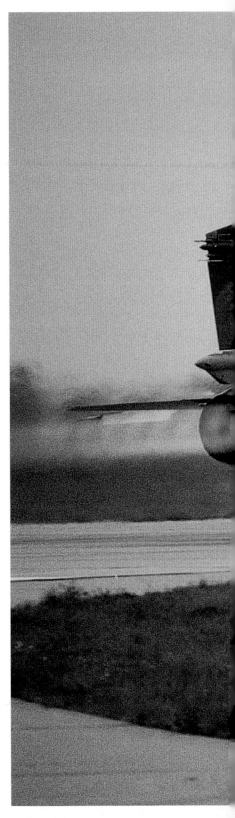

**Above** MiG-23MF '20+05' was operated by JG 9 at Peenemünde before receiving Luftwaffe codes following German reunification. The MiG-23s did not fly whilst carrying these markings, however, and like the Su-22s, they were disposed of during 1992. The only former East German combat aircraft to be adopted by the Luftwaffe were 24 MiG-29 *Fulcrums,* which are now in regular service *(Photo by F Visser/M Tabak)*

**Left** Thundering into the air trailing a reheat flame, a Hungarian Air Force MiG-23MF gets airborne from Papa Airbase in Western Hungary during August 1991. The overall size of the Hungarian Air Force (Magyar Legiero) has been drastically reduced following the installation on a new government, which imposed a 17 per cent funding cutback on expenditure. At the same time, a request was made for the removal of former Soviet forces which were stationed in Hungary *(Photo by Peter Foster)*

**Above** Mikoyan MiG-23UB parked on the flight line at Papa in Hungary during August 1991. Looking resplendent in its tactical brown/green camouflage, this aircraft also wears the new-style national markings which have been progressively applied to all aircraft remaining in service with the Hungarian Air Force *(Photo by Peter Foster)*

**Right** The peculiar patch of green paint on the nose suggests that '03' received a fresh code when the new national insignia of the Hungarian Air Force was applied to the aircraft. Note that even the ejection seat head rest is camouflaged, the paint shop people evidently doing a thorough job! Ten MiG-23MF *Flogger-Bs* are based at Papa, armed with AA-8 *Aphid* and AA-2 *Atoll* air-to-air missiles *(Photo by Peter Foster)*

**Above** No 1 Letka/1 SLP is the only Czechoslovakian Air Force unit to operate the MiG-23ML *Flogger-G* variant, and is based at Budejovice near the Austrian border. Here, '4644' is parked in front of its concrete shelter, which is well-camouflaged, with grass covering the roof and a disruptive paint scheme applied to the doors. It contrasts starkly with the unmistakable shape of NATO shelters *(Photo by F Visser/M Tabak)*

**Left** An unusual look at a MiG-23ML at Budejovice which clearly illustrates the fully-swept position of the wings and the application of the upper surface camouflage pattern. A fairly large number of stencil markings also appear to have been applied *(Photo by Peter Foster)*

**Above** MiG-27M from the 296th Fighter Bomber Regiment at Grossenhain, just north of Dresden. The unit returned to Russia during 1993, together with all other remaining Frontal Aviation units that had stayed in the former East Germany following reunification. The gloss green paint applied to the wheels seems to be standard to virtually all former Soviet combat aircraft types *(Photo by F Visser M Tabak)*

**Right** Pictured on a rain-soaked hardstanding at Mirow-Larz, MiG-27M '30' belongs to the 19th Fighter Bomber Regiment of the Russian Air Force. The unit left the former East Germany during 1993 and returned to Russia *(Photo by F Visser/M Tabak)*

## Mikoyan MiG-23ML *Flogger G*

**Dimensions:** max span 45.82 ft (13.965 m); min span 25.52 ft (7.779 m); fuselage length less nose probe 51.61 ft (15.73 m); wing area 367.5 to 401.9 ft2 (34.16 to 37.35 m²)

**Weights:** normal TOW 34,720 lb (15,750 kg); max combat TOW 40,565 lb (18,400 kg); max ferry TOW 45,570 lb (20,670 kg).

**Powerplant:** single Tumansky/Khatchatourov R-29-300 turbojet, rated at 27,560 lb (12,500 kg) with afterburning

**Armament:** one 23 mm GSh-23L twin-barrel cannon plus typical air-to-air armament of four R-60 (AA-8 *Aphid*) and two R-23R/T (AA-7 *Apex*) missiles. Typical air-to-ground armament S-8 rockets in B-8 pods or S-5 rockets in UB-32 pods, or S-24 rockets

**Performance:** max speed at altitude Mach 2.35 or 1350 knots (2500 kmh); max IAS with 16° sweep 430 knots (800 kmh); max IAS with 45° sweep 650 knots (1200 kmh); max IAS with 71° sweep 755 knots (1400 kmh); service ceiling 60,700 ft (18,500 m); max range clean 1050 nm (1950 km); max range with three 174 Imp gal (790 litre) tanks

**Above** The Russian equivalent to the USAF's F-111, the Sukhoi Su-24MR *Fencer* is a tactical bomber and reconnaissance aircraft, this particular aircraft belonging to the 11th Regiment pictured at Finow during August 1991 *(Photo by Frank Visser)*

**Left** The Su-24MR was operated by the 11th Reconnaissance Regiment at Welzow, close to the Polish border. The unit returned home to Russia in 1993, and the Su-24MR was replaced by deliveries of Su-27B *Flankers* *(Photo by Frank Vissor)*

## Sukhoi Su-24M *Fencer D*

**Dimensions:** max span 57.87 ft (17.64 m); min span 34.01 ft (10.366 m); length 80.48 ft (24.532 m)

**Weight:** TOW 87,633 lb (39,750 kg)

**Powerplant (estimated):** two Lyulka AL-21F3A turbojets, each rated at 24,700 lbs (11,200 kg) with afterburning

**Armament:** single built-in cannon of unspecified type. Guided weapons are listed as H-23M (AS-7 *Kerry*), H-25 (AS-10 *Karen*), H-28 (AS-9 *Kyle*), H-29L/T (AS-14 *Kedge*), H-59T (AS-13 *Kingbolt*), H-58 (AS-11 *Kilter*) and R-60 (AA-8 *Aphid*). Guided or unguided bombs in the range 110 to 3300 lbs (50 to 1500 kg) can be carried, as can unguided rockets in the series S-5, S-8, S-24 and S-25

**Performance:** max speed at low level Mach 1.14 or 755 knots (1400 kmh); max speed above 3300 ft (1000 m) 865 knots (1600 kmh); range clean 755 nm (1400 km); range with two PTB-3000 tanks 1540 nm (2850 km); take-off run 4250 ft (1300 m); landing run 3300 ft (1000 m)

**Above** The star of the 1992 SBAC show at Farnborough was the Tupolev Tu-22M3 *Backfire C*, making its first appearance in the West. Although the bi-annual Farnborough show has played host to all manner of bizarre and exotic aircraft designs over the course of many years, who could have predicted that a Russian long-range nuclear bomber would ever perform before the British public? *(Photo by Tim Laming)*

**Left** With a blast of power, the mighty Tu-22M3 thunders into the sky on a sunny Saturday at Farnborough. The weather for most of the 1992 'Farnborough week' was pretty bad, but thousands of spectators nevertheless headed for Hampshire to see the unique sight of Russia's huge bomber, braving the elements to stand spellbound as the *Backfire C* took to the skies *(Photo by Tim Laming)*

## Tupolev Tu-22M3 *Backfire C*

**Type:** four-seat, twin-engined variable-sweep medium bomber

**Dimensions:** max span 112.5 ft (34.3 m); min span 76.75 ft (23.4 m); overall length 130 ft (39.6 m)

**Weights:** max TOW 273,370 lb (124,000 kg)

**Powerplant (estimated):** two Kuznetsov NK-144 turbofans, each rated at 44,100 lb (20,000 kg)

**Armament:** normal warload one X-22 (AS-4 *Kitchen*) or 26,450 lb (12,000 kg) of bombs; max warload three X-22s or 52,900 lb (24,000 kg) of bombs. One flexibly-mounted 23 mm GSh-23 twin-barrel cannon in tail turret

**Performance:** max speed at altitude Mach 1.88 or 1080 knots (2000 kmh); combat radius 1080 nm (2000 km); service ceiling 43,600 ft (13,300 m); take-off speed 200 knots (370 kmh); take-off run 6560 to 6900 ft (2000 to 2100 m); normal landing speed 154 knots (285 kmh); normal landing run 3950 to 4250 ft (1200 to 1300 m)

**Left**

After getting airborne, the *Backfire C* positioned itself for a slow fly-by, with wings swept fully forward, returning minutes later to make a high-speed pass with wings fully swept, ending the flypast with a pull-up into a welcome patch of blue sky, before turning downwind to land. The display was short, but it was a show-stopper! *(Photo by Tim Laming)*

**Above** Landing gear down, wings, flaps and slats extended, the Tu-160 takes-on a rather ungainly appearance. Some 20 per cent larger than the Rockwell B-1, the *Blackjack* carries AS-15 missiles over a combat radius of almost 2000 miles. Although the aircraft has made a few public appearances in Russia, it has yet to venture overseas – like almost every other former Soviet combat aircraft, it probably will eventually *(Photo by M Bowman)*

**Left** Looking a little shabby, but undoubtedly a very serious piece of Russian technology, the Tupolev Tu-160 (better known by NATO as *Blackjack*) is the Russian equivalent of America's B-1 Lancer. Production of the aircraft has now been halted, and only 12 aircraft are currently thought to be operational *(Photo by M Bowman)*

### Tupolev Tu-160 *Blackjack*

**Type:** four-seat, four-engined variable-sweep strategic bomber
**Dimensions:** max span 182 ft (55.5 m); length 177 ft (54 m)
**Weights:** max TOW 606,000 lb (275,000 kg)
**Powerplant:** four Samara/Trud NK-321 turbofans, each rated at 55,115 lb (25,000 kg) with afterburning
**Armament:** six AS-15 *Kent* or 12 SRAM-type missiles on rotary launcher, or approx 36,000 lb (16,500 kg) of conventional bombs. Performance: max speed at altitude Mach 2.07 or 1185 knots (2200 kmh); radius of action 3950 nm (7300 km)
(all data approximate)

# B-1B Lancer

If any aircraft could be described as controversial, then Rockwell's mighty B-1 is undoubtedly in that category. Over a period of nearly 20 years, the USAF has endeavoured to introduce an advanced strategic bomber as a successor to the venerable Boeing B-52 and yet, even in 1992, the controversy surrounding the USAF's bomber force continues as politicians question the capabilities of the B-1, and the need for the B-2.

As long ago as 1957, the USAF initiated the development of a new heavy bomber, which would eventually supplement or replace the B-52. The result was the incredible North American XB-70, which quickly fell victim to technical setbacks, costs and most importantly, politics. Following its cancellation, the USAF produced a seemingly endless series of design studies, looking at potential alternatives to the XB-70, but it was not until December 1976 that the Rockwell B-1A was finally ordered into production. Designed essentially as a high-altitude supersonic bomber (but with a low-altitude subsonic capability) armed with nuclear free-fall bombs and short range attack missiles (SRAMs), the bomber was effectively killed-off by the Carter administration long before the aircraft entered operational service, although funds were made available to continue development of the design. Finally, the new Reagan government restored production of the aircraft, with an order for 100 B-1Bs configured for low-altitude subsonic nuclear delivery, but with additional secondary capabilities such as conventional bombing, maritime surveillance and cruise missile carriage.

The resurrected B-1B, later named Lancer, first flew on 18 October 1984, ahead of schedule and within budget; quite an achievement for a modern weapons system. Thanks to the continued B-1A developmental work, only eight months of test flying was required before the B-1B entered USAF service. However, this operational debut was partly due to a congressional mandate which dictated that the aircraft should enter service in 1986, and as a result the aircraft achieved IOC (Initial Operational Capability) with only 60 per cent of the necessary test flying completed, and in retrospect, this haste seems to have been responsible for many of

**Left** One of four B-1A developmental aircraft, 74-0160 is pictured at Edwards AFB, in California, during early flight trials, complete with an avionics spine modification and an eye-catching camouflage scheme. The aircraft no longer flies, but is employed as a ground instructional airframe by the Lowry TTC *(Photo by Andy Hodgson collection)*

the minor problems which have plagued the B-1 programme.

During 1987 a report from the House Armed Services Committee stated that 'The biggest problem confronting the B-1B is not its weight growth, its fuel leaks or its uncertain electronic countermeasures. The greatest problem is the Air Force itself, which exerts more effort to obscure the B-1's problems than to correct them.' Clearly, the USAF was keen to get the B-1B into service before political considerations could again destroy the whole programme. It would be unfair to suggest that the B-1 suffered more problems than any other comparable aircraft design, but with a high political profile, each 'glitch' became a critical design error, at least in the eyes of the politicians. The fuel and hydraulic systems leaked, the all-up weight continually rose as development continued, and the early supply of spare parts was woefully inadequate. The ECM system was reportedly unreliable, as was the terrain-following radar.

However, each problem was eventually overcome, and although the entire B-1B fleet has been grounded for varying periods on more than six occasions, leading some commentators to suggest that this was why the aircraft did not participate in *Desert Storm* – the real reason may simply

**Above** 74-0158, the first of four B-1 prototypes, made a total of 79 test flights (mostly for flight qualification clearances), operating from Edwards AFB, where the aircraft is pictured in a B-1B-style European camouflage, and with the fin tip removed. The aircraft is no longer in use
*(Photo by Andy Hodgson collection)*

**Above** 74-0159 was the second B-1 prototype, and it was used primarily for structural load parameter evaluation. The aircraft was later modified to act as a test machine for the B-1B programme, a role it fulfilled until 29 August 1984 when it crashed
*(Photo by Andy Hodgson collection)*

have been that the aircraft was not required – the bomber has settled into service, and functions well.

Although the Lancer was not designed primarily as a 'stealthy' aircraft (unlike the B-2), the aircraft does have a surprisingly small radar signature, reportedly only a quarter the size of the B-52's, and radar-absorbent materials (RAM) have been used in many of the aircraft's major components. Designed for low-level target penetration, the aircraft is primarily assigned to nuclear strike duties, armed with B61 or B83 bombs, or AGM-86B ALCMs (Air Launched Cruise Missile). Terrain-following radar enables the aircraft to fly at low-level automatically, with the four-man crew shielded behind curtains fitted with PLZT (Polarized Lead Zirconium Titanate) portholes, which would drastically reduce the intensity of an external light pulse. The pilot and co-pilot sit side-by-side on Douglas ACES II (Advanced Concept Ejection Seat) zero-speed/zero-altitude seats, as do the OSO (Offensive Systems Operator) and DSO (Defensive Systems Operator), who are positioned directly behind the pilot and co-pilot. Additionally, there is a 'jump seat' for an instructor pilot.

The B-1B fleet is distributed between four bases in the United States,

**Left** Nose-on view of the Lancer, illustrating the SCMS (structural Control Mode System) foreplanes, no less than six air data sensor probes, and the high-vis refuelling alignment markings, applied to assist the tanker boom operator when aligning the refuelling boom with the Lancer's receptacle. The Lancer's stalky undercarriage provides more than adequate ground clearance for the under-slung engines, and the long tail section. Maximum take-off weight is a staggering 477,000 lbs, but despite the B-1B's weight and size, the performance figures are impressive, with a maximum speed of more than 800 mph and a range of over 7000 miles *(Photo by Tim Laming)*

**Above** With 123,120 lbs of thrust sending a cloud of heat up into the Wiltshire sky, the massive bulk of the Lancer begins a take-off run along Boscombe Down's runway. Although the B-1 is a regular participant in airshow static displays, flying demonstrations are rather less common, and usually comprise of little more than a series of fly-bys *(Photo by Boudewijn Pieters)*

## Rockwell B-1B

**Wing:** span 136 ft 8.5 in (41.67 m) spread and 18 ft 2.5 in (23.84 m) swept; area 1950.0 sq ft (181.16 m²)

**Fuselage and tail:** 147 ft 0 in (44.81 m); height 34 ft 10 in (10.62 m); tailplane span 44 ft 10 in (13.67 m); wheelbase 57 ft 6 in (17.53 m); height 34 ft 10 in

**Powerplant:** four General Electric F101-GE-102 turbofans each rated at 14,600 lb dry and 30,780 lb with afterburning

**Weights:** empty equipped 192,000 lbs (88,452 kg); maximum take-off 477,000 lbs (216,367 kg)

**Fuel and load:** internal fuel 195,000 lbs (88,452 kg); maximum ordnance 75,000 lbs (34,020 kg) carried internally and 59,000 lbs (26,762 kg) carried externally

**Speed:** maximum level speed 'clean' at high altitude about 825 mph (1328 km/h); penetration speed at 200 ft (61 m) more than 600 mph (965 km/h)

**Range:** maximum range on internal fuel about 7455 miles (12,000 km)

**Performance:** service ceiling more than 50,000 ft (15,240 m)

---

under the control of Air Combat Command. The 28th Wing (37th BS and 77th BS) are based at Ellsworth AFB in South Dakota, while 'up the road' in North Dakota, the 319th Wing (46th BS) is based at Grand Forks AFB. The 96th Wing (337th BS and 338th BS) are located at Dyess AFB in Texas, while the 384th Wing (28th BS) flies from McConnell AFB in Kansas. No B-1s are based overseas, and to date, few aircraft have even made temporary overseas deployments, other than for air show appearances. One aircraft continues to fly from Edwards AFB on various test programmes.

With the demise of Strategic Air Command (SAC), and the rapid thaw in East-West relations, the 24-hour alert concept no longer applies to the B-1B Lancer wings, and Air Combat Command embraces a rather more flexible 'expeditionary' policy. This will undoubtedly lead to a gradual change in B-1B training profiles away from nuclear delivery and increasingly towards conventional attack missions. The Lancer can also be utilised for maritime surveillance and attack duties, as it is capable of carrying depth charges and AGM-84 Harpoon anti-shipping missiles. At present, the most obvious change from the days of SAC operations is a new paint scheme, replacing grey/green distruptive camouflage with an overall 'Gunship Gray' colour, complete with twin-letter tail codes as appropriate to each B-1B base. Exactly what changes lay in store for the USAF's Lancer force remain unclear. Certainly, the future of the even more controversial Northrop B-2 seems far from secure, and its eventual delivery (or possibly the non-delivery) may well have some effect on the long-term plans for B-1B

**Above** Wings, flaps and slats extended, and all four General Electric F101-GE-102 turbofans in full reheat, the mighty B-1 gets airborne. The Lancer has so far enjoyed a rather controversial career, the entire fleet having been grounded on at least six occasions due to various problems with the airframe, engines and avionics. However, despite such technical problems, there's no doubt that the B-1 is a truly awesome aircraft. The Lancer is now the main airborne element of the USAF's nuclear deterrent, with aircraft based at McConnel AFB in Kansas, Dyess AFB in Texas, Grand Forks AFB in North Dakota, and Ellsworth AFB in South Dakota *(Photo by Tim Laming)*

operations. Whatever the outcome, the Lancer has survived against the odds, and the politicians have moved-on, shifting their attentions to the B-2 and elsewhere. Perhaps now that the spotlight has finally turned away the B-1 can quiety settle into ACC service and continue the fine traditions of its mighty Boeing predecessor.

# Tornado

Conceived as a joint project between Germany, Italy and the United Kingdom, the Tornado was successfully developed into a multi-role fighter-bomber for service with the Italian Air Force, the German Air Force and Navy, and the Royal Air Force, with later export versions being delivered to Saudi Arabia.

The tri-national project was not without problems, and many commentators firmly believed that the MRCA (Multi Role Combat Aircraft) would either fail to be completed, or would become a 'Jack of all trades' and consequently 'master of none'. Of course, the history of the Tornado development programme illustrates that multi-national co-operation does sometimes work, and the aircraft is a shining example of this. The IDS (Interdictor Strike) variant, the Tornado GR.1, is a formidable bomber, matching the capabilities of even later generation aircraft such as the F-15E Strike Eagle.

The Tornado programme began during 1968 when Belgium, West Germany, Italy and the Netherlands identified their requirement for an aircraft to replace the Lockheed F-104 Starfighter, which was at that time the main fighter-bomber type. Canada and Great Britain later joined the programme, although of course, the RAF never operated the Starfighter. Great Britain's requirement was somewhat different, as after the cancel-lation of the TSR.2, the F-111K, the Anglo-French Variable-Geometry Aircraft and various other programmes, the MRCA began to look like an attractive proposition.

As costs began to increase, Belgium, Canada and the Netherlands left the MRCA programme, leaving West Germany, Italy and the UK to complete the design of both the airframe and the engine, the latter being designed and built by Turbo Union Ltd, a Rolls-Royce, MTU and Fiat joint venture. The prototype was rolled out at Manching on 8 April 1974, flying for the first time four months later on 14 August. The first operational deliveries began during 1978 when aircraft arrived at RAF Cottesmore, the home of the Trinational Tornado Training Establishment (TTTE), where Tornado crews for West Germany, Italy and the UK are trained. The TTTE operates a mixed fleet of aircraft from all three nations, which are 'pooled'. Likewise, the instructor/student relationship is also mixed so that, for

**Left** Specially arranged for an unusual photograph, a collection of No 45 Sqn (TWCU) Tornado GR.1s are seen at Honington. Parking the Tornados was the easy bit; climbing to the top of a particularly high lighting tower was the hard part. Who said photography was all fun?! *(Photo by Tim Laming)*

## Tornado GR.1

**Wing:** span (max) 45 ft 8 in (13.90 m), (min) 28 ft 2.5 in (8.59 m); area 322.9 sq ft (30.00 m²)

**Length and height**: 54 ft 9.5 in (16.70 m), 18 ft 8.5 in (5.70 m)

**Powerplant:** two Turbo-Union RB199-34R-4 Mk 101 turbofans, each rated at 8500 lbs dry and 15,000 lbs in afterburner

**Weights:** empty 28,000 lbs (12,700 kg); loaded (clean) 40,000 lbs (18,145 kg); max take-off weight 55,000 lbs (25,000 kg)

**Speed:** max speed (clean) 840 mph (1350 km/h) at 500 ft (150 m), or Mach 1.1/1385 mph (2230 km/h) at 36,090 ft (11,000m)

**Range:** tactical radius (lo-lo-lo) with external stores 450 miles (725 km), or (hi-lo-hi) with external stores 750 miles (1200 km)

example, a German instructor might fly with a British student, in an Italian Tornado!

RAF students move from the TTTE to Honington, where the Tornado Weapons Conversion Unit (No 15(R) Sqn) teaches weapon delivery techniques and tactics, prior to posting each student to an operational RAF Tornado GR.1 squadrons. These are Nos 9, 617, 27, 31, 17 and 14 Sqns, based at Marham in the UK, and Bruggen in Germany. Two further RAF squadrons (Nos 2 and 13) fly the Tornado GR.1A, a reconnaissance-configured version of the basic IDS airframe, fitted with an infra-red sensor system.

Germany's equivalent of the TWCU is Jagdbombergeschwader 38, based at Jever, and whose operational squadrons are JBGs 31, 32, 33 and 34. Additionally, the German Navy operates one wing of Tornado IDSs, a second wing having recently been disbanded and the aircraft transferred to the Luftwaffe to form a reconnaissance unit, thus allowing RF-4Es to be retired. Like the RAF, the Luftwaffe has also identified a requirement for a dedicated reconnaissance version of the Tornado IDS, and the ECR (known in Germany as the EKA - Elektronische Kampfführung und AufklÇrung) variant is now entering service as a combined defence suppression aircraft (similar to the F-4G Wild Weasel) and reconnasissance platform.

**Right** This pair of TWCU Tornado GR.1s illustrate just one of the many unusual colour schemes which have been applied to various RAF Tornado GR.1s and F.3s for anniversary celebrations, or airshow appearances. This duo were suitably decorated for a series of 1991 show appearances, one aircraft performing a flying demonstration, the other acting as a 'spare'. Thank heavens for a splash of colour! *(Photo by Tim Laming)*

**Above** Roaring through the gloom at 250 ft, a TWCU (Tornado Weapons Conversion Unit) GR.1 pulls into a starboard turn, causing water vapour to form around the fuselage. With wings fully swept, the Tornado gives a surprisingly smooth low-level ride, especially when compared to other attack aircraft *(Photo by Tim Laming)*

**Left** ZA606, proudly wearing special No 45 Sqn colours, turns away from the camera as the undercarriage retracts and the RB199 engines spool-up to full power, with afterburners selected. No 45 Sqn was formerly the shadow designation for the TWCU, but is now the shadow designation for the Multi Engine Training Squadron (Jetstreams) at Finningly – No 15 Sqn is now the TWCU's number plate *(Photo by Tim Laming)*

Italy has three operational Tornado IDS squadrons, these being No 154 Gruppo/No 6 Stormo, No 156 Gruppo/No 36 Stormo and No 155 Gruppo/No 50 Stormo. Additionally, a small number of Tornado ECRs are expected to be delivered to Italy. Export's of the Tornado have been surprisingly small, no doubt due to the relatively high cost of such a sophisticated weapons system. So far, only Saudi Arabia has purchased the aircraft, although both the Sultan of Oman's Air Force and Jordan ordered the aircraft, later cancelling their requirements. Even the USAF considered the possibility of purchasing the Tornado as a suitable replacement for its fleet of F-4G Wild Weasels, but the idea was abandoned.

**Above** Black Bomber. Shortly before No 16 Sqn disbanded at Laarbruch (re-forming as the Jaguar Operational Conversion Unit's shadow designation), ZA591/FN was treated to what is probably the most attractive 'one-off' paint scheme to have been applied to an RAF Tornado so far. The cross keys emblem reflects No 16 Sqn's former Army co-operation role ('unlocking the enemy's secrets'), while the saint figure is a reminder that the unit formed during World War 1 at St Omer *(Photo by RAF Laarbruch)*

**Left** Resplendent in the markings of No 617 'Dambusters' Sqn, this Tornado GR.1, carrying underwing fuel tanks, a Sky Shadow ECM pod and a Phimat chaff/flare dispenser is fitted out in typical RAF training spec as carried by most GR.1s on a day-to-day basis *(Photo by Tim Laming)*

The Tornado GR.1's effectiveness was put to the test for the first time during 1991 when RAF Tornados deployed to the Gulf in support of *Desert Storm*. With detachments at Tabuk and Dhahran in Saudi Arabia, and Muharraq in Bahrain, RAF crews flew some of the most dangerous missions of the war, and contributed large numbers of aircraft to the first attacks on Iraqi airfields on the first night of the conflict. Equipped with JP233 airfield denial munitions, the Tornado crews were forced to deliver their weapons at low-level over heavily-defended targets, drawing huge amounts of anti-aircraft fire and missile attacks. Consequently, a relatively large proportion of early aircraft losses were incurred by the RAF Tornado force, leading to press speculation that the Tornado was in some way

responsible for the losses, whereas it was, of course, simply the deadly nature of the operations. When RAF attack profiles later changed to medium and high level bombing (having established air superiority), the losses were negligible. In addition to RAF operations, the RSAF and Italian AF also flew Tornado attack missions over Iraq.

Extending the aircraft's multi-role concept still further, the British government opted to produce the Tornado ADV (Air Defence Variant), which shares an 80 per cent commonailty with the IDS, but with a longer fuselage designed to accommodate additional fuel reserves, and to carry four semi-recessed BAe Skyflash AAMs. The Tornado F.3 (the F.2 designation being applied to an early production batch of ADV aircraft with less-powerful engines, which are now placed in storage) was developed in response to the RAF's need for a long-range stand-off interceptor, able to combat the increasing threat from Soviet long-range bombers such as the *Backfire*.

Equipped with radar-guided missiles, the F.3 was never intended to be a traditional 'dogfighter' as such, but it is fair to say that RAF crews have never become completely accustomed to the concept of what is essentially a bomber aircraft being used for air defence. The Tornado F.3's 'bad press' deteriorated still further when details of its GEC Avionics (Marconi) Foxhunter radar were reported by the media, revealing that the RAF was far from happy with the system. Indeed, it was not until 1991/92 that much of the Tornado F.3 fleet received full production-specification radar. While it would be unfair to suggest that the RAF is still unhappy with the overall performance of the Tornado F.3, it is probably equally fair to say that deliveries of the European Fighter Aircraft are eagerly anticipated.

However, despite the Tornado F.3's less-than glorious career, the Tornado GR.1 proved beyond doubt during 1991 that it is a truly awesome weapons system, destined to remain in service with Germany, Italy and the UK for many years to come.

**Left** Otterburn, out in the wilds of northern England, is regularly used by RAF and other NATO aircraft for low-level attack training missions. A representative airfield has been cut out of the hillside, and during exercises, a steady stream of bombers deliver practice weapons at various points over the 'airfield' complex. As a Tornado GR.1 streaks overhead, and the smoke from a previous attack begins to fade, there's an excellent opportunity for recognition 'experts' to spot a Sea Vixen, a couple of Hunters, a Jet Provost and a pair of Lightnings littered around the site *(Photo by Tim Laming)*

**Above** Back under the sun shades at Muharraq, ZA491/N receives attention from the RAF groundcrew, while the pilot completes his shut-down checks and the navigator drinks a well-earned soda *(Photo by Tim Laming)*

**Left** Tornado GR.1s at Muharraq occupying a temporary dispersal revetment, constructed by Royal Engineers. The main flightline (under a sun shelter) is visible in the distance, as is the air and groundcrew 'feeder', housed inside a huge tent and known locally (for obvious reasons) as 'Billy Smarts'
*(Photo by Tim Laming)*

**Above** ZA455/EJ at Muharraq, during *Desert Storm*, illustrating the punishing effect that continual low-level missions can have upon the paint finish of a combat aircraft. The remains of a DHL Express sticker are still visible, and the original grey/green camouflage (and the national marking applied under the cockpit) is beginning to re-appear from under the sand-coloured paint *(Photo by Tim Laming)*

**Right** Proudly wearing Garfield nose art, ZA4631/Q taxies out to the runway at Muharraq. The palm tree plantation in the distance will be a familiar sight to thousands of RAF servicemen who were stationed at the base when it played host to Shackletons, Beverleys, Andovers, Vulcans, Lightnings, Britannias and many other visiting aircraft types in the 1950s and 60s *(Photo by Tim Laming)*

**Above** Rolling across the sun-baked concrete at Muharraq, Bahrain, ZD890 taxies back to the RAF Tornado flightline after completing another mission. A former RAF base, Muharraq was literally jammed full of combat aircraft (mostly RAF and USN/USMC) during *Desert Storm* *(Photo by Tim Laming)*

**Right** With an RAF Victor and a Gulf Air L-1011 in the background, ZD790/D 'Debbie' returns to the flightline at Muharraq. The RAF shared the airfield with a large number of airliners throughout the Gulf War, using an area normally occupied by Bahrain's F-5E and F-16 fighters *(Photo by Tim Laming)*

**Overleaf** Mean Machine. The evil-looking front profile of the Tornado GR.1, resplendent in desert sand camouflage and with a sharkmouth applied to the nose, carefully wrapped around the Mauser cannon port. Following months of Gulf combat, the paint is stained with oil streaks *(Photo by Tim Laming)*

**Above** One of the most heavily-used Tornado GR.1s of *Operation Granby* (the RAF's input to *Desert Storm*), ZA447/EA flew 40 missions from its base at Tabuk, Saudi Arabia. Apart from the application of a sharkmouth marking, the aircraft was temporarily named 'MiG Eater' after destroying an Iraqi combat aircraft on the ground during a bombing mission *(Photo by Tim Laming)*

**Left** Wearing appropriate nose markings ('Hello Kuwait, G'bye Iraq'), ZD890 thunders along Marham's runway after returning from Bahrain, where the aircraft participated in 28 attack missions during the Gulf War. The oil-stained paint scheme has been touched-up in parts, producing a bizarre multi-tone effect *(Photo by Tim Laming)*

**Right** Away from the desert, the gloomy skies created by countless oil fires are replaced by the more traditional British rain clouds, as a pair of Tornado GR.1s blast their way into the sky from RAF Marham. As No 55 Sqn's Victors are retired from service, more Tornado GR.1As are moving to Marham, making the airfield a major Tornado operating base *(Photo by Tim Laming)*

**Above** ZE205 'AA' was the No 65 Sqn (No 229 OCU) CO's aircraft, identified by a small pennant applied below the canopy, and a red/yellow arrowhead on the fin tip. The OCU reserve squadron number has now been changed to No 56 *(Photo by Tim Laming)*

**Right** The Defence Research Agency operates a variety of test aircraft, including Tornado GR.1 ZA326, which flies from the Royal Aerospace Establishment at Bedford on a variety of stores carriage/release and terrain following trials. The 'raspberry ripple' colour scheme is intended to make the aircraft as visually conspicuous as possible as a flight safety precaution *(Photo by Tim Laming)*

**Above** Turning hard at low-level, a Tornado F.3 from No 229 OCU demonstrates that despite media claims, the aircraft is quite a sprightly performer. However, the aircraft was designed as a stand-off interceptor, rather than a 'dogfighter'. The RAF's fighting capability will change drastically when the European Fighter Aircraft eventually enters service *(Photo by Tim Laming)*

**Right** Gear down and refuelling probe extended, a No 229 OCU Tornado F.3 is pictured during a public demonstration at RAF St Mawgan, illustrating clearly the empty Skyflash missile bays under the fuselage. Although the Tornado F.3 has received a great deal of media criticism due to an obvious inferiority in terms of manoeuvrability when compared to aircraft such as the F-15 and Su-27, any air show demonstration will illustrate clearly that the Tornado F.3 is certainly not an 'old truck'. With the right crew, it would still present a formidable defence against most fighters *(Photo by Tim Laming)*

**Above** Performing before a capacity crowd of 200,000 spectators at the 1990 Mildenhall Air Fete, No 229 OCU's 'Raspberry Ripple', piloted by Flt Lt Fred Grundy, roars over the show site, gear and wings extended, and two shocks of flame erupting from the tail pipes *(Photo by Tim Laming)*

**Left** Flt Lt Fred Grundy, the RAF's 1990 Tornado F.3 display pilot, climbs into the cockpit of his attractively-painted display mount. The open canopy illustrates the MDC (Miniature Detonating Cord), which runs through the plexiglass, and is designed to shatter when the seat ejection sequence is initiated. The rear-view mirrors for both pilot and navigator are also clearly visible *(Photo by Tim Laming)*

**Left** Canopies open and cockpits ready for a busy afternoon of flight operations, the Tornado F.3 Operational Conversion Unit (OCU) flightline at RAF Coningsby bulges at the seams with aircraft in July 1991. The F.3 OCU has recently been renumbered No 56 (Reserve) Sqn *(Photo by Tim Laming)*

**Above** No 23 Sqn's Hardened Aircraft Shelter (HAS) complex at RAF Leeming in North Yorkshire. Although fairly well-camouflaged by surrounding trees, the shelters contrast sharply with most Eastern European designs, which are much less conspicuous. Following Gulf War experience, it is perhaps questionable whether even these 'new generation' shelters afford aircraft much protection *(Photo by Tim Laming)*

**Right** View from the navigators position in a Tornado F.3 as the wingman takes fuel from a VC10's port wing HDU (Hose Drum Unit). No 11 Sqn regularly fly with 495 gal external fuel tanks (unlike the more usual 330 gal variety) and, unlike other F.3 units, do not occupy a HAS complex. The unit would disperse away from home base at Leeming in an emergency *(Photo by Tim Laming)*

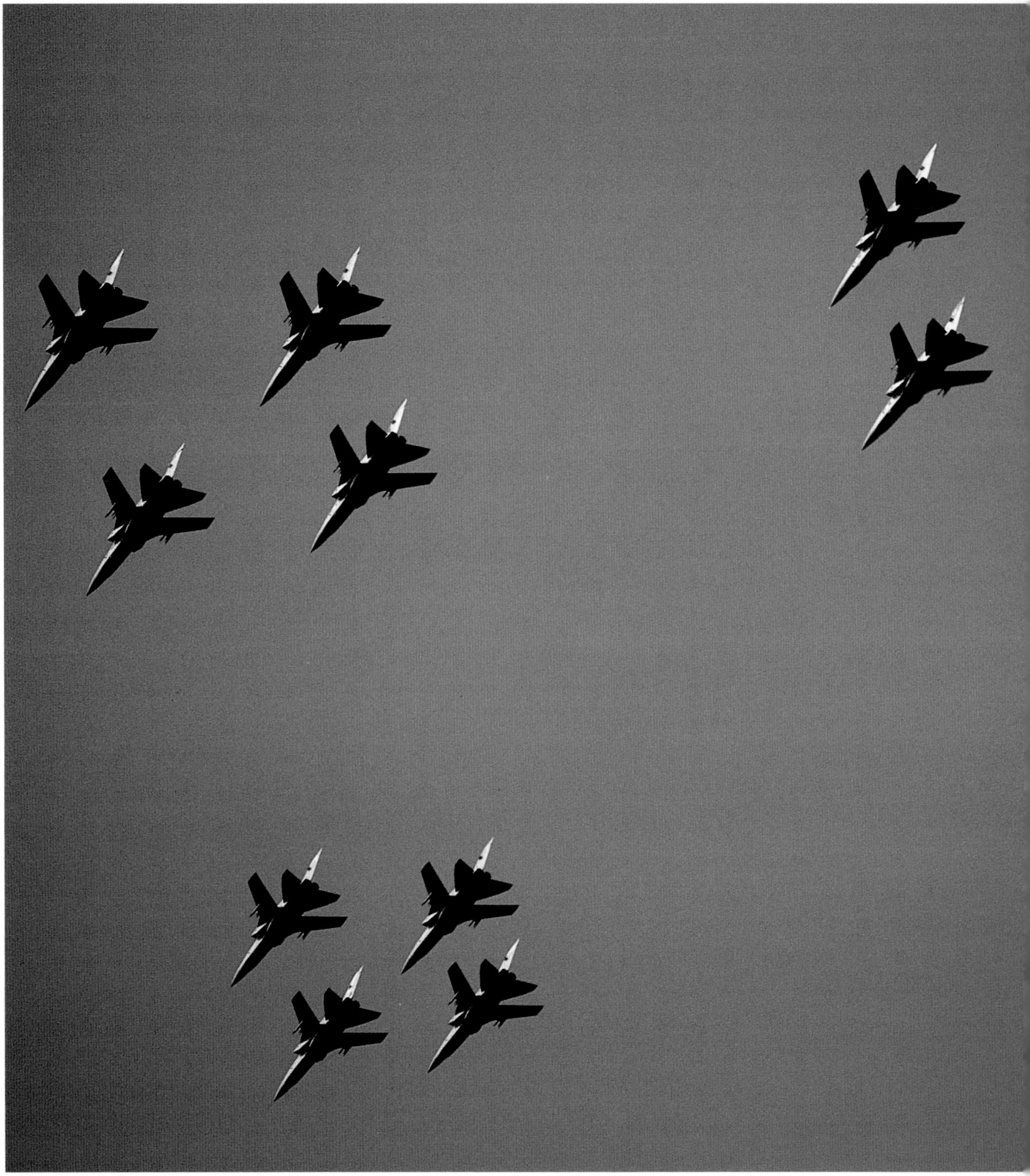

## Tornado F.3

**Wing:** span (25° sweep) 45 ft 8 in (13.90m), (68° sweep) 28 ft 2.5 in (8.59 m)

**Length and height:** 59 ft 3 in (18.06 m), 18 ft 8.5 in (5.70 m)

**Powerplant:** two Turbo-Union RB199-34R-4 Mk 104 turbofans, each rated at 9000 lbs dry and 17,000 lbs in afterburner

**Weights:** empty equipped 31,970 lbs (14,500 kg); normal loaded (four Sky Flash and four AIM-9L AAMs) 50,700 lbs (30,000 kg); max take-off weight 56,000 lbs (25,400 kg)

**Speed:** max speed 920 mph (1480 km/h) or Mach 1.2 at sea level, 1450 mph (2333 km/h) or Mach 2.2 at 40,000 ft (12,190 m)

**Range:** operational radius (combat air patrol with two 330 Imp gal/1500 litre drop tanks and allowance for two-hour loiter) 350-450 miles (560-725 kms); ferry range (with four 330 imp gal/1400 litre external tanks) 2650 miles (4265 km)

**Left** On a crisp September afternoon in 1990, the RAF celebrated the 50th anniversary of the Battle of Britain with a huge flypast over central London. Included in the flypast was a 16-ship formation of Tornado F.3s from Coningsby *(Photo by Tim Laming)*

**Above** For the 1991 air display season, a crew from No 25 Sqn was selected to perform at shows throughout the UK and Europe. Their display mount, ZE167, received an attractive paint scheme, based on the squadron's black/silver colours. As ever, the RAF officials did not think much to such exotic markings, but thankfully the aircraft did eventually appear in public and was, as you might expect, a very popular show attraction
*(Photo by Tim Laming)*

**Above right** The titles applied to the fuselage spine explain the reason for the eye-catching tail colours applied to ZE809 during 1990 *(Photo by Tim Laming)*

**Right** ZE838 received the careful attention of RAF Leeming's paint shop during 1990, appearing in an interesting colour scheme which celebrated No 25 Sqn's 75th anniversary. No 25 Sqn is one of three Tornado F.3 units based at Leeming, the others being Nos 23 and 11 Sqns *(Photo by Tim Laming)*

**Left** May 1988, and a sunny day at RAF Cottesmore sees a Luftwaffe Tornado return to the flightline after flying a TTTE (Trinational Tornado Training Establishment) mission. All German aircraft allocated to the TTTE were delivered in this attractive colour scheme, but a more mundane grey/green camouflage was later applied to all aircraft, in an effort to make the Tornado even less conspicuous. Great for tactics, but bad news for photographers!
*(Photo by Tim Laming)*

**Above** In celebration of JBG 32's 30th anniversary, Tornado '44+50' was painted in a suitably colourful paint scheme during 1988 *(Photo by Hans Schroder)*

**Left** Not many Tornados have already achieved the status of a Ground Instructional Airframe, but X-587 has done just that, its test flying days over. Now residing at Decimomannu in Sardinia, the aircraft still carries the weapons trials photographic calibration markings applied before flight tests ended. The additional pieces of artwork have been applied by visiting Italian Air Force units *(Photo by Giuseppe Fassari)*

**Left** MM7086 was one of 12 Tornado IDS variants modified for operations with the Italian Air Force in the Gulf during 1991. Unlike the RAF camouflage applied to combat aircraft in the Gulf, Italian Tornados carried a peculiar yellow finish, which was lightly sprayed over the national insignia
*(Photo by Giuseppe Fassari)*

**Above** Tornado '6-26' wears the markings of No 154 Gruppo (in red) onto which the emblem of No 6 Stormo is superimposed. The unit is based at Ghedi, and has approximately 36 aircraft assigned to it. The unusual colour of the bolt-on refuelling probe housing suggests that the attachment is not regularly carried *(Photo by Giuseppe Fassari)*

**Left** Drawn from a pool of 12 suitably modified aircraft, 10 Tornado IDSs were assigned to attack duties in the Gulf by the Italian Air Force, and were based in Abu Dhabi. Aircraft '80' received squadron markings upon arrival back in Italy, and while still wearing desert camouflage it the aircraft appeared at the 1991 Paris Air Show complete with a typical Paris tail code *(Photo by Boudewijn Pieters)*

# Rockwell International B-1B

1 Radome
2 Multi-mode phased array radar scanner
3 Low-observable shrouded scanner tracking mechanism
4 Radar mounting bulkhead
5 Radome hinge joint
6 Inflight-refuelling receptacle, open
7 Nose avionics equipment bays
8 APQ-164 offensive radar system
9 Dual pitot heads
10 Foreplane hydraulic actuator
11 Structural mode control system (SMCS) ride control foreplane
12 Foreplane pivot fixing
13 Front pressure bulkhead
14 Nose landing gear wheel bay
15 Nosewheel doors
16 Control cable runs
17 Cockpit floor level
18 Rudder pedals
19 Control column, quadruplex automatic flight control system
20 Instrument panel shroud
21 Windscreen panels
22 Detachable nuclear flash screen, all window positions
23 Co-pilot's ejector seat
24 Co-pilot's emergency escape hatch
25 Overhead switch panel
26 Pilot's emergency escape hatch
27 Cockpit eyebrow window
28 Ejector seat launch/mounting rails
29 Pilot's Weber ACES 'zero-zero' ejector seat
30 Wing sweep control lever
31 Cockpit section framing
32 Toilet
33 Nose landing gear drag brace
34 Twin landing lamps
35 Taxying lamp
36 Shock absorber strut
37 Twin nosewheels, forward retracting
38 Torque scissor links
39 Hydraulic steering control unit
40 Nosewheel leg door
41 Retractable boarding ladder
42 Ventral crew entry hatch, open
43 Nose landing gear pivot fixing

44 Hydraulic retraction jack
45 Systems Operators instrument console
46 Radar hand controller
47 Crew cabin side window panel
48 Offensive Systems Operators' ejector seat (OSO)
49 Cabin roof escape hatches
50 Defensive Systems Operators' ejector seat (DSO)
51 Rear pressure bulkhead
52 External emergency release handle
53 Under floor air conditioning ducting
54 Air system ground connection
55 External access panels
56 Avionics equipment racks, port and starboard
57 Cooling air exhaust duct
58 Astro navigation antenna
59 Forward fuselage joint frame
60 Air system valves and ducting
61 Dorsal systems and equipment duct
62 Weapons bay extended range fuel tank
63 Electric cable multiplexes
64 Forward fuselage integral fuel tank
65 Electronics equipment bay
66 Ground cooling air connection
67 Defensive avionic system transmitting antennas
68 Weapons bay door hinge mechanism
69 Forward weapons bay
70 Weapons bay doors, open
71 Retractable spoiler
72 Movable (non-structural) weapons bay bulkhead to suit varying load sizes

73 Rotary dispenser hydraulic drive motor
74 Fuel system piping
75 Communications antennas, port and starboard
76 Starboard lateral radome

77 ALQ-161 defensive avionics system equipment
78 Forward fuselage fuel tanks
79 Control cable runs
80 Rotary weapons dispenser

81 AGM-69 SRAM short-range air-to-surface missiles
82 Weapons bay door and hinge links
83 Port defensive avionics system equipment
84 Fuselage flank fuel tanks
85 Defensive avionics system transmitting antennas

86 Port lateral radome
87 Port navigation light
88 Wing sweep control screw jack
89 Wing pivot hinge fitting

90 Lateral longeron attachment joints
91 Wing pivot box carry-through
92 Wing sweep control jack hydraulic motor
93 Carry-through structure integral fuel tank
94 Upper longeron/carry-through joints

95 Starboard wing sweep control hydraulic motor
96 Wing sweep control screw jack
97 Starboard navigation light

98 Wing sweep pivot fixing
99 Wing root flexible seals
100 Aperture closing horn fairing
101 Flap/slat interconnecting drive shaft
102 Fuel pump
103 Fuel system piping

104 Starboard wing integral fuel tanks
105 Leading edge slat drive shaft
106 Slat guide rails
107 Slat screw jacks
108 Leading edge slat segments (seven), open

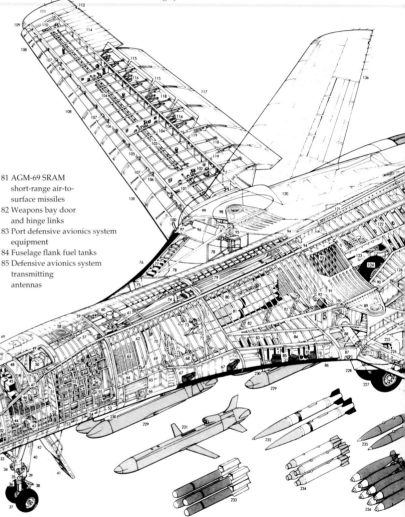

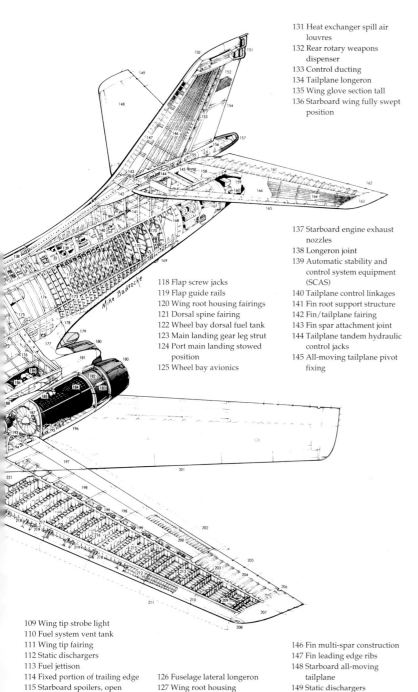

131 Heat exchanger spill air louvres
132 Rear rotary weapons dispenser
133 Control ducting
134 Tailplane longeron
135 Wing glove section tall
136 Starboard wing fully swept position

137 Starboard engine exhaust nozzles
138 Longeron joint
139 Automatic stability and control system equipment (SCAS)
140 Tailplane control linkages
141 Fin root support structure
142 Fin/tailplane fairing
143 Fin spar attachment joint
144 Tailplane tandem hydraulic control jacks
145 All-moving tailplane pivot fixing

118 Flap screw jacks
119 Flap guide rails
120 Wing root housing fairings
121 Dorsal spine fairing
122 Wheel bay dorsal fuel tank
123 Main landing gear leg strut
124 Port main landing stowed position
125 Wheel bay avionics

152 Rudder honeycomb construction
153 Rudder powered hinges
154 Two-segment upper rudder
155 Rudder automatic stability and control system equipment (SCAS)
156 Tail warning radar equipment
157 Tailcone radome fairing
158 Lower rudder segment
160 Defensive avionics system transmitting antennas
161 Tailplane trailing edge rib construction
162 Static dischargers
163 Tailplane tip fairing
164 Multi-spar tailplane
165 Port all-moving tailplane
166 Tailplane skin panelling
167 ALQ-161 defensive avionics system equipment racks
168 Vortex generators
169 Ventral communications antennas
170 Fin attachment fuselage
171 Rear fuselage integral fuel tank
172 Tank pressurization nitrogen bottle
173 Rear fuselage lower longeron
174 Rear weapons bay bulkhead
175 Weapons bay doors
176 Engine nacelle mounting beam
177 Radar absorbent material (RAM) coated skin panelling
178 Trailing edge wing root fairing
179 Aft external cruise missile carriage
180 Port engine afterburner nozzles
181 Wing glove section tail fairing
182 Afterburner ducting
183 Variable area afterburner nozzle control jacks
184 General Electric F101-GE-102 afterburning turbofan engines
185 Engine bleed air trappings
186 Bleed air pre-cooler
187 Inlet compressor faces
188 Wing glove articulated sealing plates
189 Nacelle duct framing
190 Hydraulic reservoirs
191 Engine fire suppression
192 Garret Auxiliary Power Unit (APU), port and starboard
193 Airframe mounted engine accessory equipment gearbox
194 Electrical system generator

195 Engine fuel system equipment, fully automatic digital engine control
196 Engine cowling panels
197 Port single-slotted Fowler-type flaps
198 Port spoiler panels (four)
199 Spoiler hydraulic jacks
200 Flap rib construction
201 Port wing fully swept position
202 Flap down position
203 Trailing edge ribs
204 Fixed portion of trailing edge
205 Static dischargers
206 Fuel jettison
207 Port wing tip fairing
208 Wing tip strobe light
209 Fuel vent tank
210 Port leading edge slat segments
211 Slat open position
212 Slat rib construction
213 Port wing integral fuel tank
214 Rear spar
215 Lower wing skin/stringer panel
216 Wing rib construction
217 Front spar
218 Leading edge slat guide
219 Slat screw jacks
220 Slat drive shaft
221 Wing skin panelling
222 Nacelle inlet S-duct
223 Inlet anti-radar reflection internal vanes
224 Boundary layer spill duct
225 Port engine air inlets
226 Hinged inlet side panel variable capture area
227 Four-wheel main landing gear bogie, inward and aft retracting
228 Engine inlet central divider
229 External carriage 14 × ALCM maximum
230 Missile pylons
231 AGM-86B Air Launched Cruise Missile (ALCM) deployed configuration, maximum of eight missiles internally
232 AGM-69 SRAM air-to-surface missiles, 24 internally
233 B-28 or B-43 free fall nuclear weapons (eight)
234 B-61 or B-83 free fall nuclear weapons (24)
235 Mk 84 907-kg (2000 lb) HE bombs (24)
236 Mk 82 227-kg (500 lb) HE bombs (84)

109 Wing tip strobe light
110 Fuel system vent tank
111 Wing tip fairing
112 Static dischargers
113 Fuel jettison
114 Fixed portion of trailing edge
115 Starboard spoilers, open
116 Spoiler hydraulic jacks
117 Single-slotted Fowler-type flap, down

126 Fuselage lateral longeron
127 Wing root housing
128 Engine bleed air duct
129 Ventral retractable air scoop
130 Fuel cooling heat exchanger

146 Fin multi-spar construction
147 Fin leading edge ribs
148 Starboard all-moving tailplane
149 Static dischargers
150 Fin tip antenna fairing
151 Defensive avionics system receiving antennas

# Panavia Tornado GR.Mk 1

1 Air data probe
· 2 Radome
3 Lightning conductor strip
4 Terrain following radar antenna
5 Ground mapping radar antenna
6 Radar equipment bay hinged position
7 Radome hinged position
8 IFF aerial
9 Radar antenna tracking mechanism
10 Radar equipment bay
11 UHF/TACAN aerial
12 Laser Ranger and Marked Target Seeker (Ferranti), starboard side
13 Cannon muzzle
14 Ventral Doppler aerial
16 Angle of attack transmitter
16 Canopy emergency release
17 Avionics equipment bay
18 Front pressure bulkhead
19 Windscreen rain dispersal air ducts
20 Windscreen (Lucas-Rotax)
21 Retractable, telescopic, inflight refuelling probe
22 Probe retraction link
23 Windscreen open position, instrument access
24 Head-up display, HUD (Smiths)
25 Instrument panel
26 Radar 'head-down' display
27 Instrument panel shroud
28 Control column
29 Rudder pedals
30 Battery
31 Cannon barrel
32 Nose wheel doors
33 Landing/taxiing lamp
34 Nose undercarriage leg strut (Dowty-Rotol)
35 Torque scissor links
36 Twin forward retracting nose wheels (Dunlop)
37 Nose wheel steering unit
38 Nose wheel leg door
39 Electrical equipment bay
40 Ejection seat rocket pack
41 Engine throttle levers
42 Wing sweep control lever
43 Radar hand controller
44 Side console panel
45 Pilot's Martin-Baker Mk 10 ejection seat
46 Safety harness
47 Ejection seat headrest

48 Cockpit canopy cover (Kopperschmidt)
49 Canopy centre arch
50 Navigator's radar displays
51 Navigator's instrument panel and weapons control panels
52 Footrests
53 Canopy external latch
54 Pitot head
55 Mauser 27 mm cannon
56 Ammunition feed chute
57 Cold air unit ram air intake
58 Ammunition tank
59 Liquid oxygen converter
60 Cabin cold air unit
61 Stores management system computer
62 Port engine air intake
63 Intake lip
64 Cockpit framing
65 Navigator's Martin-Baker Mk 10 ejection seat
66 Starboard engine air intake
67 Intake spill duct
68 Canopy jack
69 Canopy hinge point
70 Rear pressure bulkhead
71 Intake ramp actuator linkage
72 Navigation light
73 Two-dimensional variable area intake ramp doors
74 Intake suction relief doors
75 Wing glove Krüger flap
76 Intake bypass air spill ducts
77 Intake ramp hydraulic actuator
78 Forward fuselage fuel tank
79 Wing sweep control screw jack
80 Flap and slat control drive

81 Wing sweep, flap and slat central control unit and motor (Microtechnica)
82 Wing pivot box integral fuel tank
83 Air system ducting
84 Anti-collision light
85 UHF aerials
86 Wing pivot box carry-through, electron beam welded titanium structure
87 Starboard wing pivot bearing
88 Flap and slat telescopic drive shafts
89 Starboard wing sweep control screw jack
90 Leading edge sealing fairing
91 Wing root glove fairing
92 External fuel tank capacity 330 Imp gal (1500 litres)

93 AIM-9L Sidewinder air-to-air self-defence missile
94 Canopy open position
95 Canopy jettison unit
96 Pilot's rear view mirrors
97 Starboard three-segment leading edge slat, open
98 Slats crew jacks
99 Slat drive torque shaft
100 Wing pylon swivelling control rod
101 Inboard pylon pivot bearing
102 Starboard wing integral fuel tank
103 Wing fuel system access panels
104 Outboard pylon pivot bearing
105 Marconi 'Sky-Shadow' ECM pod
106 Outboard wing swivelling pylon
107 Starboard navigation and strobe lights

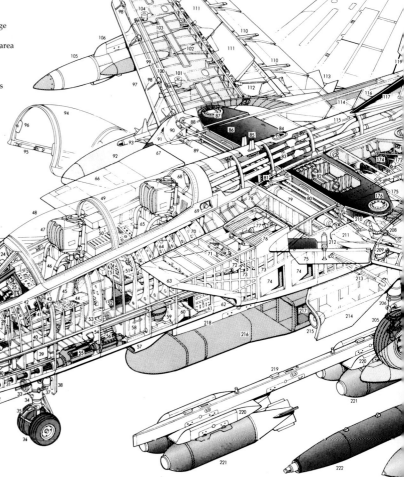

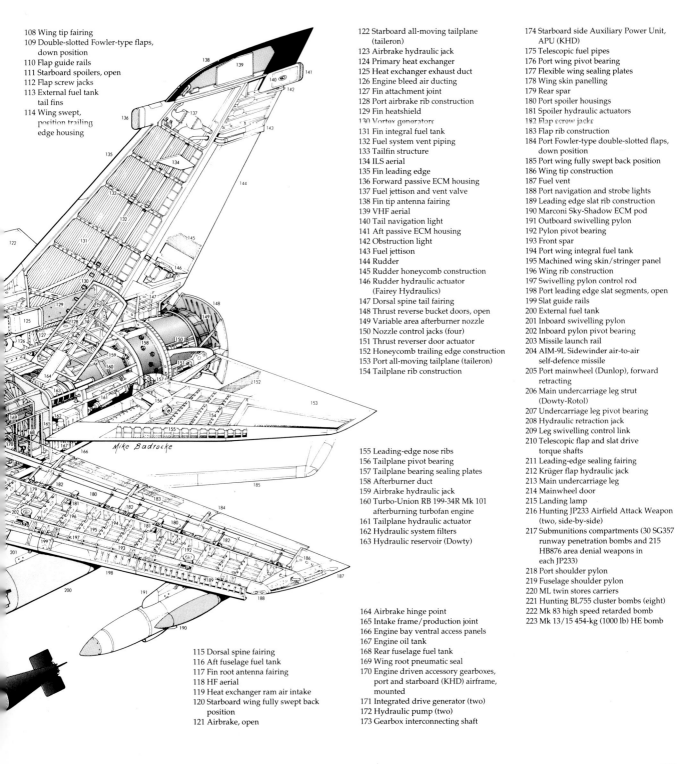

108 Wing tip fairing
109 Double-slotted Fowler-type flaps, down position
110 Flap guide rails
111 Starboard spoilers, open
112 Flap screw jacks
113 External fuel tank tail fins
114 Wing swept, position trailing edge housing

115 Dorsal spine fairing
116 Aft fuselage fuel tank
117 Fin root antenna fairing
118 HF aerial
119 Heat exchanger ram air intake
120 Starboard wing fully swept back position
121 Airbrake, open

122 Starboard all-moving tailplane (taileron)
123 Airbrake hydraulic jack
124 Primary heat exchanger
125 Heat exchanger exhaust duct
126 Engine bleed air ducting
127 Fin attachment joint
128 Port airbrake rib construction
129 Fin heatshield
130 Vortex generators
131 Fin integral fuel tank
132 Fuel system vent piping
133 Tailfin structure
134 ILS aerial
135 Fin leading edge
136 Forward passive ECM housing
137 Fuel jettison and vent valve
138 Fin tip antenna fairing
139 VHF aerial
140 Tail navigation light
141 Aft passive ECM housing
142 Obstruction light
143 Fuel jettison
144 Rudder
145 Rudder honeycomb construction
146 Rudder hydraulic actuator (Fairey Hydraulics)
147 Dorsal spine tail fairing
148 Thrust reverse bucket doors, open
149 Variable area afterburner nozzle
150 Nozzle control jacks (four)
151 Thrust reverser door actuator
152 Honeycomb trailing edge construction
153 Port all-moving tailplane (taileron)
154 Tailplane rib construction

155 Leading-edge nose ribs
156 Tailplane pivot bearing
157 Tailplane bearing sealing plates
158 Afterburner duct
159 Airbrake hydraulic jack
160 Turbo-Union RB 199-34R Mk 101 afterburning turbofan engine
161 Tailplane hydraulic actuator
162 Hydraulic system filters
163 Hydraulic reservoir (Dowty)

164 Airbrake hinge point
165 Intake frame/production joint
166 Engine bay ventral access panels
167 Engine oil tank
168 Rear fuselage fuel tank
169 Wing root pneumatic seal
170 Engine driven accessory gearboxes, port and starboard (KHD) airframe, mounted
171 Integrated drive generator (two)
172 Hydraulic pump (two)
173 Gearbox interconnecting shaft

174 Starboard side Auxiliary Power Unit, APU (KHD)
175 Telescopic fuel pipes
176 Port wing pivot bearing
177 Flexible wing sealing plates
178 Wing skin panelling
179 Rear spar
180 Port spoiler housings
181 Spoiler hydraulic actuators
182 Flap screw jacks
183 Flap rib construction
184 Port Fowler-type double-slotted flaps, down position
185 Port wing fully swept back position
186 Wing tip construction
187 Fuel vent
188 Port navigation and strobe lights
189 Leading edge slat rib construction
190 Marconi Sky-Shadow ECM pod
191 Outboard swivelling pylon
192 Pylon pivot bearing
193 Front spar
194 Port wing integral fuel tank
195 Machined wing skin/stringer panel
196 Wing rib construction
197 Swivelling pylon control rod
198 Port leading edge slat segments, open
199 Slat guide rails
200 External fuel tank
201 Inboard swivelling pylon
202 Inboard pylon pivot bearing
203 Missile launch rail
204 AIM-9L Sidewinder air-to-air self-defence missile
205 Port mainwheel (Dunlop), forward retracting
206 Main undercarriage leg strut (Dowty-Rotol)
207 Undercarriage leg pivot bearing
208 Hydraulic retraction jack
209 Leg swivelling control link
210 Telescopic flap and slat drive torque shafts
211 Leading-edge sealing fairing
212 Krüger flap hydraulic jack
213 Main undercarriage leg
214 Mainwheel door
215 Landing lamp
216 Hunting JP233 Airfield Attack Weapon (two, side-by-side)
217 Submunitions compartments (30 SG357 runway penetration bombs and 215 HB876 area denial weapons in each JP233)
218 Port shoulder pylon
219 Fuselage shoulder pylon
220 ML twin stores carriers
221 Hunting BL755 cluster bombs (eight)
222 Mk 83 high speed retarded bomb
223 Mk 13/15 454-kg (1000 lb) HE bomb

Mike Badrocke

# Grumman (General Dynamics) EF-111 A Raven

1 Pitot head
2 Radome
3 AN/APQ-160 navigation radar antenna (redundant attack mode)
4 Twin AN/APQ-110 terrain-following radar scanners
5 Antenna controller
6 Glideslope aerial
7 Scanner tracking mechanism
8 Radar scanner module
9 Scanner mounting bulkhead
10 Ventral ILS aerial
11 UHF comm/Tacan aerial
12 Hinged nose compartment access doors
13 Avionics equipment racks, radar
14 Forward ALQ-137 low and mid band antenna
15 Forward avionics bay upper decking
16 Liquid oxygen converter, starboard side
17 ADF aerial
18 Windscreen rain dispersal airducts
19 Avionics equipment, tactical jamming system (TJS)
20 Flush VOR localizer aerial
21 Cockpit pressurization relief valve
22 Angle of attack transmitter
23 Nose wheeldoors
24 Twin nosewheels, forward retracting
25 Steering control jack
26 Electro-luminescent formation lighting strip
27 Nose landing gear wheel bay
28 Pressurized escape capsule joint frame
29 Underfloor impact attenuation air bags (four)
30 Rudder pedals
31 Control column
32 Instrument panel
33 Instrument panel shroud
34 Curved windscreen panels
35 Canopy arch
36 Upward hinged cockpit canopy covers
37 Electronic warfare officer's seat
38 Rear bulkhead console
39 Circuit breaker panels
40 Canopy jack
41 Headrest
42 Adjustable seat mounting
43 Pilot's seat
44 Canopy latch
45 Wing sweep control lever
46 Engine throttle levers
47 Side console panel
48 Provisions and survival equipment stowage
49 Conditioned air ducting
50 Weapons/avionics equipment bay door open
51 Electrical system equipment
52 Forward fuselage fuel tank, total fuel capacity 18,919 litres (4,998 US gal)
53 Cockpit rear pressure bulkhead

54 Escape capsule recovery parachute container
55 Parachute attachment/release link
56 Emergency oxygen bottles (two)
57 Self righting airbag (two)
58 Airbag pressurization bottle
59 Upper UHF/IFF aerial
60 Escape capsule aft flotation bags, port and starboard
61 Stabilising and brake parachute stowage
62 Escape capsule chine section frame construction
63 Pitch stabilizers, port and starboard
64 Pressure refuelling connection
65 Fuel system control panel
66 Port navigation light
67 Boundary layer splitter plate
68 Port engine air intake
69 Movable intake spike fairing (Triple Plow 1 intake system)
70 Boundary layer duct ram air intake to conditioning system
71 Fuselage chine section integral fuel tank
72 Inflight-refuelling receptacle, open
73 ALQ-137 low/mid/high band receiver and ALR-62 forward radar warning receiver antennas, port and starboard
74 Starboard navigation light
75 UHF/Tacan aerial
76 Wing sweep control screw jacks, port and starboard
77 Anti-collision light
78 Boundary layer spill air louvres
79 Wing pivot box integral fuel tank
80 Fuselage upper longerons
81 Flap and slat drive electro-hydraulic motor
82 Wing pivot box carry-through
83 Electro-luminescent formation lighting strip
84 Starboard wing pivot bearing
85 Wing sweep control horn
86 Wing root rotating glove section, open
87 Starboard external fuel tank
88 Slat drive gearbox
89 Data link pod
90 Swivelling external stores pylons
91 Pylon attachment joints
92 Pylon angle control link
93 Fuel system piping
94 Starboard wing integral fuel tank
95 Slat drive shaft
96 Geared slat guide rails
97 Leading edge slat segments, open
98 Starboard wing fully forward (16-deg sweep) position
99 Wing tip position light
100 Electro luminescent formation lighting strip
101 Static dischargers

102 Full-span double-slotted Fowler-type flaps, down position
103 Outboard roll control spoiler/lift dumper
104 Spoiler hydraulic actuators
105 Inboard roll control spoiler/lift dumper, de-activated at sweep angles greater than 45 degrees
106 Flap guide rails
107 Flap drive shaft
108 Screw jack
109 Wing root auxiliary flap
110 Auxiliary flap actuator
111 Angled flap drive shaft
112 Starboard engine intake trunking
113 Dorsal cable and systems ducting
114 HF aerial spine fairing
115 Diagonal rib
116 Starboard Pratt & Whitney TF30-P-3 engine
117 Fuselage flank fuel tank
118 Wing root pneumatic seal
119 Rear fuselage dorsal fuel tank
120 Starboard wing fully swept (72.5 degree) position
121 Starboard all-moving tailplane
122 Static dischargers
123 Aft ALR-62 radar warning receiver
124 Fin honeycomb leading edge panel
125 HF aerial shunt
126 Fin integral vent tank
127 Multi-spar tailfin construction
128 ALQ-99 band 2 antenna
129 ALQ-99 band 1 antenna

130 Fin tip System Integrated Receiver (SIR) pod attachment joint
131 SIR pod forward radome
132 Forward ALQ-99 receiving antennas
133 RF divider
134 ALQ-99 receivers
135 ALR-62 antenna switching unit
136 TRU-79 induction transmitters
137 ALR-23 cryogenic converter
138 Lateral ALQ-99 antennas

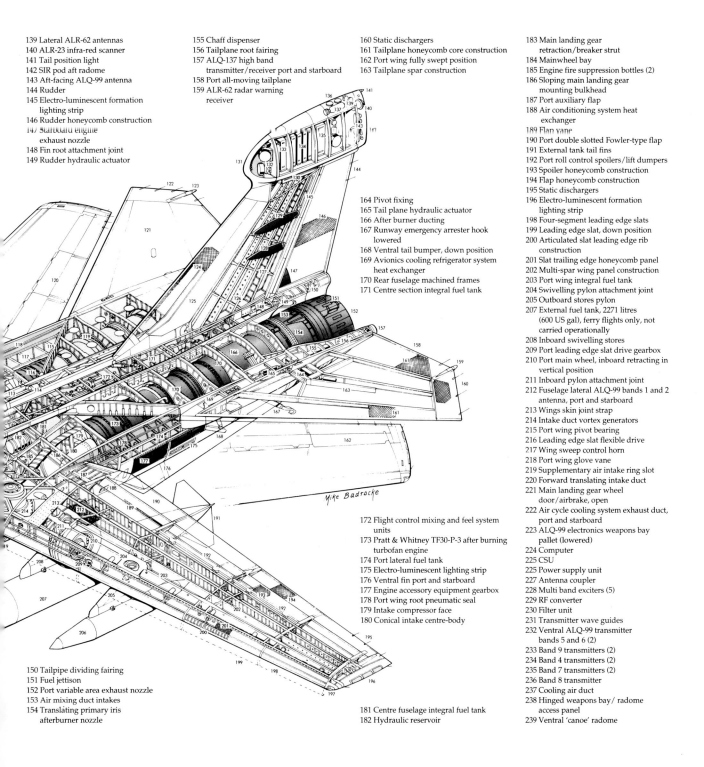

139 Lateral ALR-62 antennas
140 ALR-23 infra-red scanner
141 Tail position light
142 SIR pod aft radome
143 Aft-facing ALQ-99 antenna
144 Rudder
145 Electro-luminescent formation
    lighting strip
146 Rudder honeycomb construction
147 Starboard engine
    exhaust nozzle
148 Fin root attachment joint
149 Rudder hydraulic actuator

155 Chaff dispenser
156 Tailplane root fairing
157 ALQ-137 high band
    transmitter/receiver port and starboard
158 Port all-moving tailplane
159 ALR-62 radar warning
    receiver

160 Static dischargers
161 Tailplane honeycomb core construction
162 Port wing fully swept position
163 Tailplane spar construction

164 Pivot fixing
165 Tail plane hydraulic actuator
166 After burner ducting
167 Runway emergency arrester hook
    lowered
168 Ventral tail bumper, down position
169 Avionics cooling refrigerator system
    heat exchanger
170 Rear fuselage machined frames
171 Centre section integral fuel tank

172 Flight control mixing and feel system
    units
173 Pratt & Whitney TF30-P-3 after burning
    turbofan engine
174 Port lateral fuel tank
175 Electro-luminescent lighting strip
176 Ventral fin port and starboard
177 Engine accessory equipment gearbox
178 Port wing root pneumatic seal
179 Intake compressor face
180 Conical intake centre-body

150 Tailpipe dividing fairing
151 Fuel jettison
152 Port variable area exhaust nozzle
153 Air mixing duct intakes
154 Translating primary iris
    afterburner nozzle

181 Centre fuselage integral fuel tank
182 Hydraulic reservoir

183 Main landing gear
    retraction/breaker strut
184 Mainwheel bay
185 Engine fire suppression bottles (2)
186 Sloping main landing gear
    mounting bulkhead
187 Port auxiliary flap
188 Air conditioning system heat
    exchanger
189 Flap vane
190 Port double slotted Fowler-type flap
191 External tank tail fins
192 Port roll control spoilers/lift dumpers
193 Spoiler honeycomb construction
194 Flap honeycomb construction
195 Static dischargers
196 Electro-luminescent formation
    lighting strip
198 Four-segment leading edge slats
199 Leading edge slat, down position
200 Articulated slat leading edge rib
    construction
201 Slat trailing edge honeycomb panel
202 Multi-spar wing panel construction
203 Port wing integral fuel tank
204 Swivelling pylon attachment joint
205 Outboard stores pylon
207 External fuel tank, 2271 litres
    (600 US gal), ferry flights only, not
    carried operationally
208 Inboard swivelling stores
209 Port leading edge slat drive gearbox
210 Port main wheel, inboard retracting in
    vertical position
211 Inboard pylon attachment joint
212 Fuselage lateral ALQ-99 bands 1 and 2
    antenna, port and starboard
213 Wings skin joint strap
214 Intake duct vortex generators
215 Port wing pivot bearing
216 Leading edge slat flexible drive
217 Wing sweep control horn
218 Port wing glove vane
219 Supplementary air intake ring slot
220 Forward translating intake duct
221 Main landing gear wheel
    door/airbrake, open
222 Air cycle cooling system exhaust duct,
    port and starboard
223 ALQ-99 electronics weapons bay
    pallet (lowered)
224 Computer
225 CSU
225 Power supply unit
227 Antenna coupler
228 Multi band exciters (5)
229 RF converter
230 Filter unit
231 Transmitter wave guides
232 Ventral ALQ-99 transmitter
    bands 5 and 6 (2)
233 Band 9 transmitters (2)
234 Band 4 transmitters (2)
235 Band 7 transmitters (2)
236 Band 8 transmitter
237 Cooling air duct
238 Hinged weapons bay/radome
    access panel
239 Ventral 'canoe' radome

# Mikoyan-Gurevich
# MiG-23MF
## *Flogger-G*

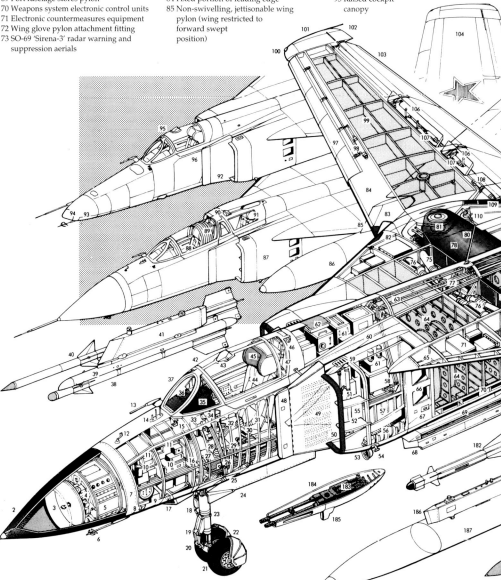

1 Pitot tube
2 Radome
3 Flat dish radar scanner
4 Scanner tracking mechanism
5 'High Lark' J-band pulse Doppler radar module
6 'Swift Rod' ILS aerial
7 Radar mounting bulkhead
8 Cooling air scoop
9 Ventral Doppler navigation aerial
10 Weapons system avionics equipment
11 Nose compartment access doors
12 Yaw vane
13 Dynamic pressure probe (q-feel)
14 SRO-2 'Odd Rods' IFF antenna
15 Temperature probe
16 Cockpit front pressure bulkhead
17 Ventral laser range finder
18 Nose wheel steering control
19 Torque scissor links
20 Pivoted axle beam
21 Twin aft-retracting nosewheels
22 Nosewheel spray/debris guards
23 Shock absorber strut
24 Nose wheel doors
25 Hydraulic retraction jack
26 Angle of attack transmitter
27 Rudder pedals
28 Control column
29 Three position wing sweep control lever
30 Engine throttle lever
31 Cockpit section framing
32 Ejection seat firing handles
33 Radar 'head-down' display
34 Instrument panel
35 Instrument panel shroud
36 Weapons sighting unit head up display
37 Armoured glass windscreen panel
38 AA-2 *Atoll* (K-13A) infra-red homing air-to-air missile
39 Missile bunch rail
40 AA-2-2 *Advanced Atoll* radar homing air-to-air missile
41 Wing glove pylon
42 Cockpit canopy cover upward hingeing
43 Electrically heated rear view mirror
44 Pilot's 'zero-zero' ejection seat
45 Ejection seat headrest/drogue parachute container
46 Canopy hinge point
47 Canopy hydraulic jack
48 Boundary layer splitter plate
49 Boundary layer ramp bleed
50 Port engine air intake
51 Adjustable intake ramp screw jack control
52 Intake internal flow fences
53 Retractable landing/taxying lamp, port and starboard
54 Pressure sensor, automatic intake control system
55 Variable area intake ramp doors
56 Intake duct framing

57 Ventral cannon ammunition magazine
58 Control rod linkages
59 Intake ramp bleed air ejector
60 Boundary layer spill duct
61 Avionics equipment
62 ADF sense aerial
63 Tailplane control rods
64 Forward fuselage fuel tanks
65 Wing glove fairing
66 Intake duct suction relief doors
67 Ground power and intercom sockets
68 Twin missile carrier/launch unit
69 Port fuselage stores pylon
70 Weapons system electronic control units
71 Electronic countermeasures equipment
72 Wing glove pylon attachment fitting
73 SO-69 'Sirena-3' radar warning and suppression aerials

74 Wing sweep control horn
75 Screw jack wing sweep rotary actuator
76 Twin hydraulic motors
77 Central combining gearbox
78 Wing pivot box carry-through unit (welded steel construction)
79 Pivot box integral fuel tank
80 VHF aerial
81 Wing pivot bearing
82 Starboard 'Sirena-3' radar warning and suppression aerials
83 Extended-chord saw tooth leading edge
84 Fixed portion of leading edge
85 Non-swivelling, jettisonable wing pylon (wing restricted to forward swept position)

86 Jettisonable fuel tank (800 litre/176 Imp gal capacity)
87 Nose section of MiG-23U *Flogger-C* tandem seat trainer
88 Student pilot's cockpit
89 Folding blind flying hood
90 Rear seat periscope, extended
91 Instructor's cockpit
92 MiG-23BN *Flogger-F* dedicated ground attack variant
93 Radar ranging antenna
94 Laser ranging nose fairing
95 Raised cockpit canopy

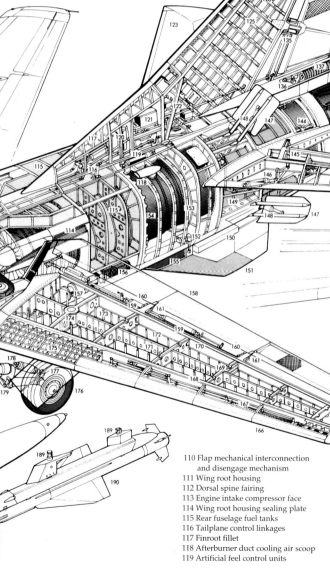

96 Armoured fuselage side panels
97 Starboard wing leading edge flap (lowered)
98 Leading edge flap hydraulic actuator
99 Starboard wing integral fuel tank (total fuel capacity 5750 litres / 1265 Imp gal)
100 Starboard navigation light
101 Wing fully forward (16-degree sweep) position
102 Static discharger
103 Full-span three-segment plain flap (lowered)
104 Starboard wing immediate (45-degree sweep) position

105 Starboard wing full (72-degree sweep) position
106 Two-segment spoilers/lift dumpers (open)
107 Spoiler hydraulic actuators
108 Flap hydraulic jack
109 Wing glove flexible seal

120 Control system hydraulic accumulator
121 Artificial feel and autopilot controls
122 Tailplane trim controls
123 Starboard all-moving tailplane
124 Fin leading edge

134 Honeycomb core construction
135 Rudder hydraulic actuators, port and starboard
136 Parachute release links
137 Brake parachute housing
138 Split conical fairing parachute doors
139 Variable-area afterburner nozzle
140 Fixed tailplane tab
141 Honeycomb core trailing edge panel
142 Static discharger
143 Port all-moving tailplane construction
144 Afterburner nozzle control jacks (six)
145 Tailplane pivot bearing
146 Tailplane actuator
147 Airbrakes (four) upper and lower surfaces
148 Airbrake hydraulic jacks
149 Afterburner duct heat shroud
150 Ventral fin, folded (landing gear down) position
151 Ventral fin down position
152 Screw jack fin actuator
153 Fin attachment fuselage main frame
154 Tumansky R-29B afterburning turbojet engine
155 Lower UHF aerial
156 Engine accessory equipment compartment
157 Air conditioning system equipment
158 Port plain flap
159 Spoiler actuators
160 Port spoilers/lift dumpers
161 Flap guide rails
162 Fixed spoiler strips
163 Static discharger
164 Wing tip fairing
165 Port navigation light
166 Port leading edge flap
167 Leading edge flap control linkage
168 Front spar
169 Wing rib construction
170 Rear spar
171 Auxiliary centre spar
172 Wing skin support struts
173 Port wing integral fuel tank
174 Wing pylon attachment fitting
175 Leading edge rib construction
176 Port main wheel
177 Main wheel door/debris guard
178 Shock absorber strut
179 Pivoted axle beam
180 Articulated mainwheel leg strut
181 Mainwheel leg doors
182 AA-8 *Aphid* (R-60) short range air-to-air missile
183 GSh-23L twin-barrel 23 mm cannon
184 Ventral cannon pack
185 Gun gas venting air scoop
186 Fuselage centre line pylon
187 Ventral fuel tank (800 litre/176 Imp gal capacity)
188 *Apex* missile launch rail
189 Launch rail attachment hardpoints
190 AA-7 *Apex* (R-23) long-range air-to-air missile

Mike Badrocke

110 Flap mechanical interconnection and disengage mechanism
111 Wing root housing
112 Dorsal spine fairing
113 Engine intake compressor face
114 Wing root housing sealing plate
115 Rear fuselage fuel tanks
116 Tailplane control linkages
117 Finroot fillet
118 Afterburner duct cooling air scoop
119 Artificial feel control units

125 Tailfin construction
126 Short wave ground control communications aerial
127 Fin tip UHF aerial fairing
128 ILS aerial
129 ECM aerial
130 'Sirena-3' tail warning radar
131 Tail navigation light
132 Static discharger
133 Rudder

125

# Grumman
# F-14A Tomcat

1 Pitot tube
2 Radar target horn
3 Glass-fibre radome
4 IFF aerial array
5 Hughes AWG-9 flat plate radar scanner
6 Scanner tracking mechanism
7 Ventral ALQ-100 antenna
8 Gun muzzle blast through
9 Radar electronics equipment bay
10 AN/ASN-92 inertial navigation unit
11 Radome hinge
12 In-flight refuelling probe (extended)
13 ADF aerial
14 Windscreen rain removal air duct
15 Temperature probe
16 Cockpit front pressure bulkhead
17 Angle of attack transmitter
18 Formation lighting strip
19 Cannon barrels
20 Nosewheel doors
21 Gun gas vents
22 Rudder pedals
23 Cockpit pressurisation valve
24 Navigation radar display
25 Control column
26 Instrument panel shroud
27 Kaiser AN/ANG-12 head-up display
28 Windscreen panels
29 Cockpit canopy cover
30 Face blind seat firing handle
31 Ejection seat headrest
32 Pilot's Martin-Baker GRU-7A
   ejection seat
33 Starboard side console panel
34 Engine throttle levers
35 Port side console panel
36 Pitot static head
37 Canopy emergency release handle
38 Fold out step
39 M61A1 Vulcan 20 mm six-barrel
   rotary cannon
40 Nose undercarriage leg strut
41 Catapult strop link
42 Catapult strop, launch position
43 Twin nosewheels
44 Folding boarding ladder
45 Hughes AIM-54A Phoenix
   air-to-air missile (6)
46 Fuselage missile pallet
47 Cannon ammunition
   drum (675 rounds)
48 Rear boarding step
49 Ammunition feed chute
50 Armament control panels
51 Kick-instep
52 Tactical information display hand
   controller
53 Naval Flight Officer's
   instrument console
54 NFO's ejection seat

55 Starboard intake lip
56 Ejection seat launch rails
57 Cockpit aft decking
58 Electrical system controller
59 Rear radio and electronics
   equipment bay
60 Boundary layer bleed air duct
61 Port engine intake lip
62 Electrical system relay controls
63 Glove vane pivot
64 Port air intake
65 Glove vane housing
66 Navigation light
67 Variable area intake ramp doors
68 Cooling system boundary layer duct ram
   air intake
69 Intake ramp door hydraulic jacks
70 Air system piping
71 Air data computer
72 Heat exchanger
73 Heat exchanger exhaust duct
74 Forward fuselage fuel tanks
75 Canopy hinge point
76 Electrical and control system ducting
77 Control rod runs
78 UHF/TACAN aerial
79 Glove vane hydraulic jack
80 Starboard glove vane extended
81 Honeycomb panel construction
82 Navigation light
83 Main undercarriage wheelbay
84 Starboard intake duct spill door
85 Wing slat/flap flexible drive shaft
86 Dorsal spine fairing
87 Fuselage top longeron
88 Central flap/slat drive motor
89 Emergency hydraulic generator
90 Bypass door hydraulic jack
91 Intake bypass door
92 Port intake ducting
93 Wing glove sealing horn

99 UHF data link/IFF aerial
100 Honeycomb skin panelling
101 Wing glove stiffeners/dorsal fences
102 Starboard wing pivot bearing
103 Slat/flap drive shaft gearbox
104 Starboard wing integral fuel tank
   (total internal fuel capacity 2364 US
   gal/8951 l)
105 Leading edge slat drive shaft
106 Slat guide rails
107 Starboard leading edge slat
   segments (open)
109 Low-voltage formation lighting
110 Wing tip fairing
111 Outboard manoeuvre flap segments
   (down position)
112 Port roll control spoilers
113 Spoiler hydraulic Jacks
114 Inboard, high lift flap (down position)
115 Inboard flap hydraulic jack
116 Manoeuvre flap drive shaft
117 Variable wing sweep screw jack
118 Starboard main undercarriage
   pivot fixing
119 Starboard engine compressor face
120 Wing glove sealing plates
121 Pratt & Whitney TF30- P-412
   afterburning turbofan
122 Rear fuselage fuel tanks
123 Fuselage longeron joint
124 Control system artificial
   feel units
125 Tailplane control rods

94 Flap/slat telescopic drive shaft
95 Port wing pivot bearing
96 Wing pivot carry-through (electron beam
   welded titanium box construction)
97 Wing pivot box integral fuel tank
98 Fuselage longeron/pivot box attachment
   joint

126 Starboard engine bay
127 Wing glove pneumatic seal
128 Fin root fairing
129 fin spar attachment joints
130 Starboard fin leading edge

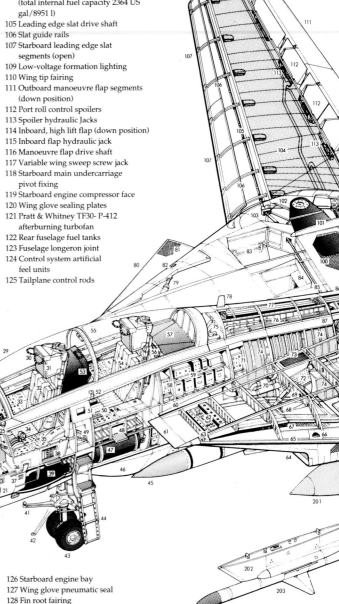

131 Starboard all-moving tailplane
132 Starboard wing(fully swept position)
133 AN/ALR-45 tail warning radar antenna
134 Fin aluminium honeycomb skin panel construction
135 Fin-tip aerial fairing
136 Tail navigation light
137 Electronic countermeasures antenna (ECM)
138 Rudder honeycomb construction
139 Rudder hydraulic jack
140 Afterburner ducting
141 Variable area nozzle control jack
142 Airbrake (upper and lower surfaces)
143 Airbrake hydraulic jack
144 Starboard engine exhaust nozzle
145 Anti-collision light
146 Tail formation light
147 ECM aerial
148 Port rudder
149 Beaver tail fairing
150 Fuel jettison pipe
151 ECM antenna
152 Deck arrester hook (stowed position)
153 AN/ALE-29A chaff and flare dispensers
154 Nozzle shroud sealing flaps
155 Port convergent/divergent afterburner exhaust nozzle
156 Tailplane honeycomb construction
157 AN/ALR-45(V) tail warning radar antenna
158 Tailplane boron fibre skin panels
159 Port wing (fully swept position)
160 All-moving-tailplane construction
161 Tailplane pivot fixing
162 Jet pipe mounting
163 Fin/tailplane attachment mainframe
164 Cooling air louvres
165 Tailplane hydraulic jack
166 Hydraulic system equipment pack
167 Formation lighting strip
168 Oil cooler air intake
169 Port ventral fin
170 Engine accessory compartment
171 Ventral engine access doors
172 Hydraulic reservoir
173 Bleed air ducting
174 Port engine bay
175 Intake compressor face
176 Wing variable sweep screw jack
177 Main undercarriage leg strut
178 Hydraulic retraction jack
179 Wing skin panel
180 Fuel system piping
181 Rear spar
182 Flap hinge brackets
183 Port roll control spoilers
184 Flap leading edge eyebrow seal fairing
185 Port manoeuvre flap honeycomb
186 Wing tip fairing construction
187 Low-voltage formation lighting
188 Port navigation light
189 Wing rib construction
190 Port wing integral fuel tank
191 Front spar
192 Leading edge rib construction
193 Slat guide rails
194 Port leading edge slat segments, open
195 Slat honeycomb construction
196 Port mainwheel
197 Torque scissor links
198 Main undercarriage front bracing strut
199 Mainwheel door
202 Sparrow missile launch adaptor
203 AIM-7F Sparrow air-to-air missile
204 Wing glove pylon attachment
205 Cranked wing glove pylon
206 Sidewinder missile launch rail
207 AIM-9C Sidewinder air-to-air missile
208 Phoenix launch pallet
209 AIM-54A Phoenix air-to-air missile

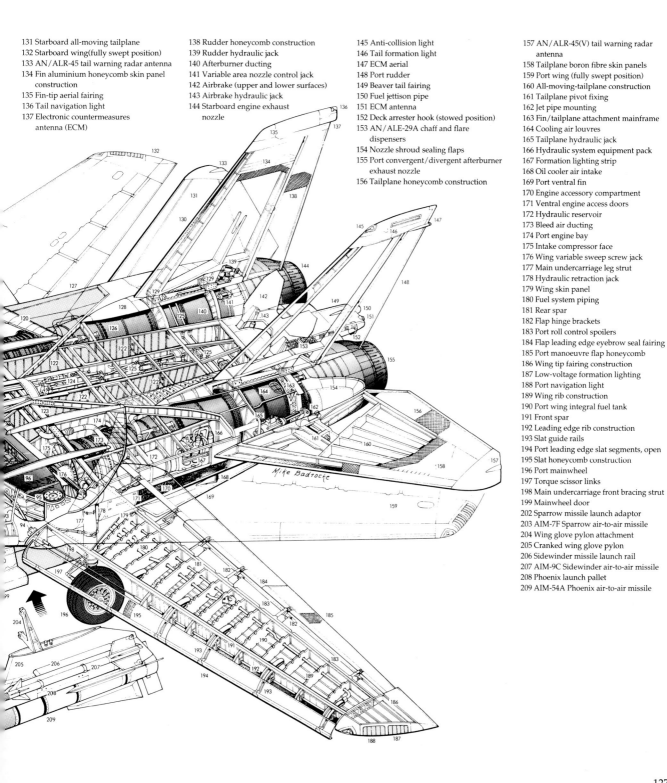

Mike Badrocke

**Above** Streaming-in over the runway threshold at RAF Fairford, a pair of Italian Air Force Tornados arrive at the 1991 International Air Tattoo. One aircraft wears standard service camouflage, whilst the other still retains the desert sand paint scheme which was applied to Italian Tornados deployed to the Gulf during *Desert Storm (Photo by Boudewijn Pieters)*